Lyndon

Lyndon

Richard Harwood and Haynes Johnson

A 𝔚𝔞𝔰𝔥𝔦𝔫𝔤𝔱𝔬𝔫 𝔓𝔬𝔰𝔱 **Book**

PRAEGER PUBLISHERS

NEW YORK · WASHINGTON · LONDON

PRAEGER PUBLISHERS
111 Fourth Avenue, New York, N.Y. 10003, U.S.A.
5, Cromwell Place, London SW7 2JL, England

Published in the United States of America in 1973
by Praeger Publishers Inc.

Third printing, 1973

© 1973 by Richard Harwood and Haynes Johnson

LIBRARY OF CONGRESS CATALOGING IN PUBLICATION DATA

Harwood, Richard.
    Lyndon.

    Bibliography.
    1. Johnson, Lyndon Baines, Pres. U. S., 1908–1973.
I. Johnson, Haynes Bonner, 1931–   joint author.
E847.H34   973.923′092′4 [B]   73-5226

Printed in the United States of America

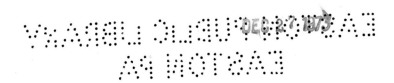

This book is for our children—
Helen, John, Richard, David,
Katherine, Stephen, Sarah, and Elizabeth

Contents

Acknowledgments

The *Washington Post* files contain memoranda of private meetings with Lyndon Johnson that, by themselves, provide a running chronicle of his presidency and total tens of thousands of words. In nearly every case where we quote from Johnson's conversations, these memoranda provide our source. Out of all these records of his sessions with the press, only the account of one of the last times those of us at the *Post* saw Lyndon Johnson at an extraordinary 5-hour luncheon in April, 1970, has been published previously—and that in much abbreviated form immediately after his death.

We wish to thank, especially, two of our colleagues at the *Post*, Carroll Kilpatrick and Chalmers M. Roberts, for kindly making available their own files of their numerous private meetings with the President. We are grateful to Charles B. Seib, managing editor of the Washington *Star-News*, for providing additional private material. And we owe a special debt to Benjamin C. Bradlee, executive editor, and Howard Simons, managing editor, of the *Washington Post*, both for urging us to write this book and for making it possible for us to do it.

We also wish to thank the following publishers for their permission to quote from these works: Holt, Rinehart and Winston, *The Vantage Point*, by Lyndon Baines Johnson, Copyright © 1971 by HEC Public Affairs Foundation (New York: 1971); Alfred A. Knopf, *The Tragedy of Lyndon Johnson*, by Eric F. Goldman (New York: 1969); Atlantic-Little, Brown, *A Political Education*, by Harry McPherson (Boston: 1972); and the New American Library, *Lyndon B. Johnson: The Exercise of Power*, by Rowland Evans and Robert Novak, Copyright © by Rowland Evans and Robert Novak (New York: 1966). Two other books cited are *The Lyndon Johnson Story*, by Booth Mooney (New York: Farrar, Straus, 1964), and *First Rough Draft*:

A Journalist's Journal of Our Times, by Chalmers M. Roberts (New York: Praeger, 1973). Sam Houston Johnson and Marvin Josephson Associates gave us permission to quote from *My Brother Lyndon* (New York: Cowles, 1970), and the Lyndon Baines Johnson Library in Austin, Texas, graciously provided us with many photographs of the President, for which we wish to express our thanks. Herbert L. Block kindly permitted use of cartoons from the *Washington Post*.

William Snead, director of photography for the *Post*, was a full partner in the production of this book. He selected the photographs it contains and aided in its design and layout. From the beginning of our project, Lois Decker O'Neill of Praeger Publishers encouraged us in every way and was a sensitive and skillful editor. We want to thank both of them and also our associates at the *Post*, Bridget Gallagher and Miranda D. Lorraine, without whose research and manuscript assistance this book literally could not have been produced.

RICHARD HARWOOD
HAYNES JOHNSON

Washington, D.C.
May, 1973

Lyndon

"So Damned Formidable"

In the overblown rhetoric of American politics, when a mediocre man dies he immediately is hailed as good, a good man is described as great, and a "great" leader is said to belong to the immortals of the endless ages. Those who spoke in memoriam of Lyndon Johnson invariably cast him in monumental terms. He was larger than life. He was tragically misunderstood. He was a true servant of the people, a man of the soil, a son of humble origins who never lost the common touch, an original American, a lasting link between North and South, East and West. He was the greatest legislator ever to stride through the halls of Congress, perhaps the most skillful, powerful political practitioner of them all. A great President to be sure, certainly the best friend of the blacks since Lincoln. He was all these things and more, a legend, a giant, a Bunyanesque figure, a creature of the elements. "It is tempting to say that losing President Johnson is like losing a part of our national landscape," said Adlai Stevenson's son and namesake. "But Lyndon Johnson was always too restless and fast-moving to be described as a mere landmark. Losing him is like losing part of the weather."

In the timing and manner of his death, the orators and writers found omens and ironies and deeper significance: His passing marked the end of an era of bitterness and division, it signaled the dawning of a new day of peace and reconciliation. In death, the former President was rendered the respect and love he was so often denied in life.

"He almost had to be dead before you could assess the man," said his aide and confidante Horace Busby. "He was so damned formidable."

Lyndon would have loved these tributes. He always was a man of excesses with a penchant for Texas-sized hyperbole. Some day he will have his biographer, and it will take the talents of a Mark Twain to capture him. Indeed,

Twain would have understood him well. He had written of those raucous, boasting, lusty men of the Southwest as American primitives. "Whoo-oop!" Twain quoted one of them as saying. "I'm the original iron-jawed, brass-mounted, copper-bellied corpse-maker from the wilds of Arkansas! . . . Look at me and lay low and hold your breath, for I'm 'bout to turn myself loose!" They were, as Twain said, "prodigious braggarts; yet, in the main, honest, trustworthy, faithful to promises and duty, and often picturesquely magnanimous."

Lyndon Johnson was of that line. Prodigious and picturesque, yes. Magnanimous, sometimes. Complicated, always. A spinner of tall tales, the most vivid and original storyteller in the White House since Lincoln. No one who sat with him, or saw him up close in private, could forget him. The trouble was that in his lifetime—and it will be even more difficult for the historians—it often seemed impossible to sift fact from fiction. Lyndon seemed to realize that himself.

The last time we saw him, during a memorable five-hour private luncheon, he told one surprising version of major historical events after another. At one point, perhaps noticing our look of incredulity, he remarked that he was a complex person. Then, tapping his forehead, he said: "Sometimes I don't even know what's going on up there."

We make no claim of being able to unravel all the contradictions and complexities. We are reporters, not historians, and we have no illusions that we can offer a definitive portrait of Lyndon Johnson and his times. What we are attempting is a close, and critical, look at Lyndon, the man, and LBJ, the politician. Over the years we watched him. We traveled with him, wrote about him, incurred his wrath and commendation, saw evidence of his vulgarities and fondness for biological humor and bathroom behavior, his rages and cruelties, as well as his touching moments of generosity and, yes, nobility.

Our first impression remains indelible. It was a political rally in Washington, sometime in the 1950s, dreary in its way, as they all are. All the war horses of the Democrats had turned out: Harry Truman; "Mister Sam" Rayburn, the tough, balding, flinty, somewhat inscrutable Speaker of the House; Averell Harriman, an ambassador who wanted to become President. There were others who wanted to become President, senators all of them—Hubert Humphrey of Minnesota, Stuart Symington of Missouri, John Kennedy of Massachusetts. Then there was LBJ. He took the podium, leaned forward, and launched into a loud, stemwinding stump speech. He flailed his arms. He pounded the lectern. He shouted until he was hoarse. He leaned forward to watch the crowd. You could see the veins bulging out on his neck. No one was surprised; that was the way the rangy majority leader regaled the faithful in Texas.

Years later, another Johnson and another speech. It was his first address to Congress as President. Soft, subdued, almost soulful. Seeing him, who could remember him as anything other than the quiet, fatherly figure he seemed that day?

His first trip as President was marked by those same illuminating flashes of the private Johnson behind the public one that we would see in later trips

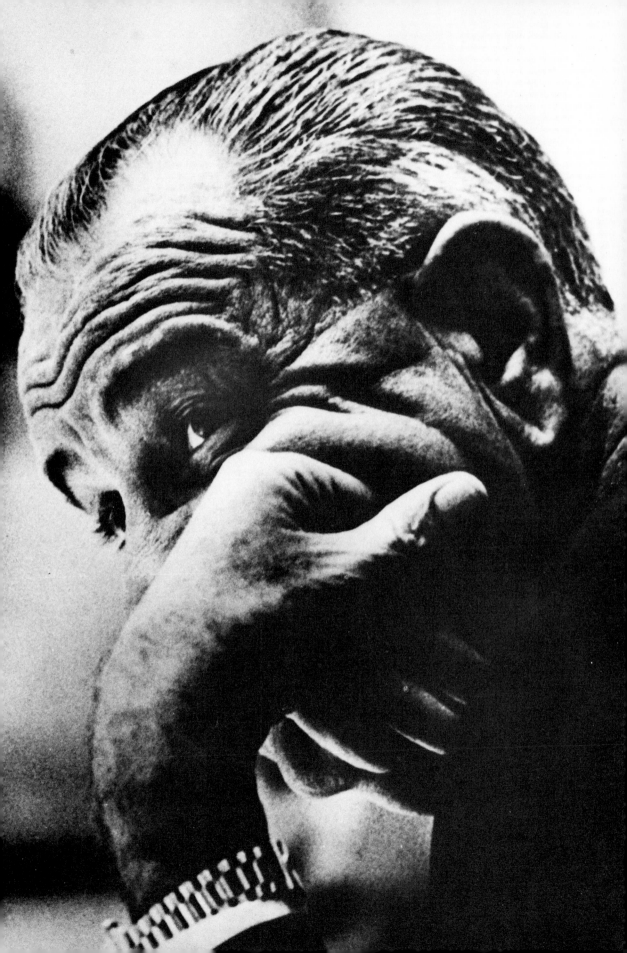

and conversations with him. For months after the Kennedy assassination Lyndon had remained in the White House, waiting out the transition period between mourning and action. Then, in the early spring of 1964, he took to the country. He was a force unleashed. Restless, searching, he charged into crowds, grasping hands and beaming at the squeals and screams his presence elicited while his Secret Service men stood by in despair. He moved across the land, from town to city to state capital, declaring war on poverty and promising to banish it from the nation. Late in the day his helicopter arrived in Inez, Kentucky, a hamlet tucked away in the Appalachians. His wife was exhausted. She sat in the car, holding a bouquet of roses, grateful for a moment's respite while her husband charged through the crowds. As he walked forward, shaking hands left and right, he noticed his wife wasn't at his side.

"Where's Bird?" he said in a low tone to a Secret Service agent at his side.

"She's behind us in the limousine, Mr. President."

"Tell her to get out here and walk with me," the President said, still in the same low tone, still moving forward shaking hands.

"She's very tired, Mr. President," the agent began.

"Get Bird out here and tell her I want her to walk with me," the President snapped.

Minutes later, his wife joined him, smiling faintly, still carrying her roses.

Lyndon Johnson could be that way.

When he died, James Reston of the *New York Times* recalled that Lyndon

. . . loved the camera. No President collected more photographs of himself and his visitors than Mr. Johnson; but the tape recorder was really the instrument he should have used. For he gave himself to his visitors, and historians will never be able to sort out the glory and the tragedy unless they manage to collect the stories, listen to the tape recorders and forget the television, which

was his downfall, and somehow hear him talking endlessly about his problems, his cunning contrivances, his feeling for the Congress, his love of his country, and particularly his affection for his lovely and remarkable wife, and his hard-scrabble land in Texas.

We share Reston's view both of the man and of his glory and tragedy. It will be years before all the papers of Lyndon Johnson's presidency are opened to scholars. We have not had, nor have we sought, access to these private papers. Instead we have relied on our own impressions and the memories of others who were close to Lyndon Johnson. As reporters, we covered him and most of the major events of his time. We reported on his Senate days, on his vice presidential and presidential campaigns, on the civil rights movement, on the Dominican Revolution, on the field from Vietnam, on the home front during that harsh 1968 political year which included Robert Kennedy's assassination, and on national developments during the post-Johnson presidential years.

The *Washington Post* files contain voluminous and detailed accounts of private sessions with Lyndon, of Lyndon in the White House, at the ranch, at lunch, at dinner, on a plane in this country or abroad. These memoranda recorded remarks that, in the peculiar nature of President and press, were always off the record and never for attribution. Reading them now, even in their rough form, we are struck with the sharp picture of the private, and real, Lyndon that emerges—as opposed to the public impression that grew up around him during his stormy presidency.

Here we see Lyndon raging at the press, the Kennedys, the intellectuals: Lyndon saying of one prominent columnist "You don't have to see him; you can smell him,"; Lyndon describing Bob Kennedy standing before his desk, his Adam's apple "going like a Yo-Yo" while he, the President, "watched him like a hawk watches a chicken" as he told Kennedy he was being eliminated from vice-presidential consideration; Lyndon telling stories of Franklin Roosevelt, the man he always measured himself against, of Sam Rayburn and Texas and the frontier, and of the place he knew perhaps better than anyone and dominated for so long—Washington, D.C.

Through the generosity of other journalists and political friends, we have been able to add other private accounts of Lyndon. Some are arresting and disturbing: the stories he told, both in the White House and later, of his recurring dreams, of his fears of losing control, of his prowling the dark White House early in the morning with a flashlight, and of his feeling that he could rely on no one, not even his most trusted aides. Others are sad. Perhaps the most poignant come from those last years at the ranch when as an older, wounded man, knowing, his friends insist, that he was going to die, and feeling ignored and forgotten, he poured out his soul to a young woman who was, of all things, an Easterner, a scholar, and an intellectual.

It will be years, of course, before he finally finds his proper place in history. Lyndon Johnson, that dominant, flawed, forceful figure who came to presidential power on a clap of thunder and a beat of drums, all his life aroused strong emotion and controversy. When he left office quietly, discredited, disliked, and disparaged, he retired to his ranch to await a more compassionate judgment.

We remember him as a man who once said he didn't want everybody to love him, as his enemies often claimed, he just wanted everybody to like him —and we remember him as a President of the United States, one of the mightiest and most maligned of them all.

LBJ: The Making of an Operator

We rarely know our public men. The "definitive" histories are never written until long after they are dead. What we know of them in their lifetimes is the imperfect knowledge that is made of myth and gossip, the half-truths of political rhetoric, the shorthand of journalism, the fleeting, simplified images that flash on our television screens. And when they have died, the myths and the symbols are elevated to truth in the ceremonial mournings that follow—John Kennedy, the Prince of Camelot; Harry Truman, the Enduring Common Man; Dwight Eisenhower, the Simple Soldier of Freedom.

While he lived, Lyndon Johnson floated in and out of our consciousness under many labels—New Dealer, Wheeler Dealer, Crude Texan, Friend of the Poor and the Black, Warmonger, Tyrant, Fool, Imperialist. At his death, old Wright Patman of Texas, who knew him and his father, saw in him the qualities of a "folk hero out of a saga from our frontier days—larger than life, like Davy Crockett or one of the storied martyrs who died at the Alamo." Nicholas von Hoffman, the iconoclastic columnist of the *Washington Post*, was overwhelmed by the gargantuan appetites and capacities of the man:

. . . You were immoderate and greedy. You outdid all the rest of us hungry Americans for reaching out and grabbing, fingers always stretched for grasping, but now they're saying after your death that you divided America, left her all split and bleeding. It is true that if ever a man had a reach which exceeded his grasp, it was you, you wicked old devil, but you redeemed this country even while dropping us, plop!, in the middle of the Vietnam Big Muddy.

You fought our Second Civil War and carried out our Second Reconstruction . . . You were so impulsive. You tried to solve social problems like a drunken hardware wholesaler trying to snag girls in a Paris nightclub . . .

21

but God bless you for it . . . You were a big 'un, Lyndon.

Horace Busby, who served this "folk hero," this "wicked," "impulsive" man for twenty-five years, who wrote many of his speeches, who sat by him in the great moments of his life and in the days before he died, chuckles at some of the legends and some of the rhetoric Lyndon inspired. Busby, too, came out of Texas, and he is not unaware of how myths sometimes get born.

There were, for example, presidential speeches full of allusions to the "poor caliche soil" whence Lyndon Baines Johnson had sprung, speeches that evoked the image of a disadvantaged rustic lad—a twentieth century Lincoln—who had overcome the poverty of his origins and who had risen through true grit to the leadership of the Western World. Those speeches, by Busby's wry recollection, were not written by any of the Texans on Johnson's staff but by Richard Goodwin, a Harvard *summa cum laude* who had clerked for Justice Felix Frankfurter, had been brought into politics by John Kennedy, and was a spiritual and cultural stranger to the realities of Texas and its politicians.

The realities of Lyndon Johnson's origins in Texas are full of ambiguities. He was at once the political figure and President who could boast publicly of his humble origins and who could also say privately with a touch of envy or bitterness that "my ancestors were teachers and lawyers and college presidents and governors when the Kennedys in this country were still tending bar."

The biographical facts do not entirely resolve these ambiguities, but it is clear that in the context of his time and place he was born with certain advantages. He was a child of middle-class, small-town America. His mother —Rebekah Baines Johnson—was bookish, greatly ambitious for her son, and possessed of certain literary pretensions. In her later years she exhibited her florid writing style in a recollection of herself and Lyndon:

The mother looked into her son's brown eyes, seeing in them not only the quick intelligence and fearless spirit that animated her husband's flashing eyes, but also the deep purposefulness and true nobility that had shone in her father's steady brown eyes.

A family friend has described her as a "kind of early century hippie. She thought she had married beneath herself. She was pregnant all the time (there were five children) and laid around in bed writing poetry." As an outlet for her small talents and larger ambitions she would spend all the days that she could at the local newspaper office, writing perishable prose, away from home and the children.

The father, Sam Ealy Johnson, taught school, farmed, bought and sold land, speculated in cotton, and took his family through good times and bad. In the family portraits, he and Lyndon could pass as twins. They were tall and gaunt with huge ears, thick eyebrows, prominent chins. They shared, too, certain personality characteristics. The father, like the son in later years, was short-tempered, quick to find fault, hypertensive. Both were to die of heart attacks.

Sam Johnson was a successful politician by the lights of Johnson City, al- though his ambitions never ran beyond the brawling Texas legislature where he served several terms and made political connections that were to help Lyndon to get to Washington at an early age. He was a talker and a story teller with a fondness for whisky.

"We had great ups and downs in our family," Lyndon recalled near the end of his life. "One year things would go just right. We'd all be riding high in Johnson City terms, so high in fact that on a scale of A-F we'd be up there with the As. But then two years later we'd lose it all. The cotton my father had bought for 44 cents a pound had dropped to 6 cents a pound and with it we had dropped to the bottom of the heap. When things got bad like this, Father used to drink even more than usual. I think alcoholism's got a tendency to run in families; some men take to women; others to food; still others to drink. Well, for my father and for his friends it was always drink."

Sam Houston Johnson, who became something of a wayward relative in later life, had the same recollections. In his book *My Brother Lyndon* he said:

For a writer searching for a dramatic rags-to-riches angle, that picture of Lyndon trudging along a dusty country road with a cardboard suitcase is understandably tempting; but it gives a false impression about our family's economic condition. Though he was never a wealthy man, our daddy was always able to provide for his family, sometimes more lavishly than others but never bordering on poverty. Our home was certainly no mansion by any definition, yet it was probably the nicest house in town while we were growing up.

Of his father's drinking habits, Sam Houston wrote:

Lyndon sometimes objected to certain aspects of my daddy's life style— drinking, for example . . . My daddy, being a state legislator, would frequently meet some of his political cronies at the saloon and spend a few hours there discussing the latest developments at the state capitol. Well, that was what Lyndon objected to: Old Demon Rum.

The Johnsons lived as cattlemen, land buyers, farmers—and as politicians. The Baineses were lawyers, preachers, teachers, doctors—and also politicians. They were well established when Lyndon was born near Johnson City on August 27, 1908. On his birth, it was said many years afterward, his Grandfather Johnson went galloping off on horseback, proclaiming: "A United States Senator was born this morning—my grandson." But like so much else in the Johnson story, this anecdote appears to have been somewhat inflated. The grandfather, the record shows, later in life did write a daughter to say, "I have a mighty fine grandson, smart as you find them. I expect him to be a United States Senator before he is 40."

Lyndon's childhood, so far as is known, was not remarkably eventful, although it is likely that psychohistorians will one day find meaning and significance in the tensions between his parents, in the conflict of their values, desires, and ambitions, and in the very different outcome of the careers of the other Johnson children. But his biographers—the real biographers, not the pamphleteers and propagandists who wrote such one-sided accounts of him— do have an intriguing period of his early life to unravel.

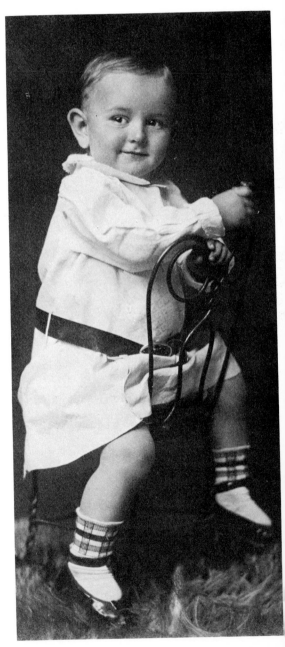

Sam and Rebekah
and their son

An all-"A" student— except in deportment

Lyndon (fifth from left, top) and high school class

With fellow teachers in Texas and (below, left) on a Mexican honeymoon

Sam Johnson, as legislator and bidding LBJ farewell

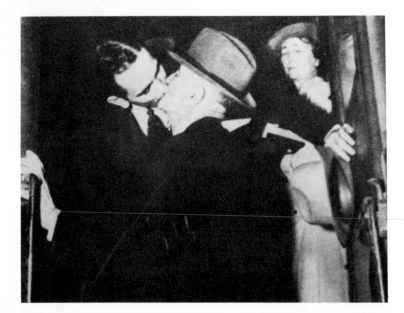

Lyndon's favorite photo: meeting his hero FDR—he kept this picture with him wherever he went

When he was still in his teens, Lyndon took to the highways. He had graduated from the Johnson City high school at the age of fifteen, the vale-dictorian of the six-member class. Then he dropped out for a year afterward, as millions of middle-class students were to do a half-century later. His formal campaign material noted only that he worked his way west to California by taking odd jobs. He was an elevator operator, a car washer, a handyman in a cafe. What happened to him on those journeys, what experiences colored his outlook, no one really knows.

"Up and down the Pacific Coast I tramped," he said years later, "washing dishes, waiting on tables, doing farm work when it was available and growing thinner and more homesick." He was not entirely on his own. His mother had a cousin in Los Angeles, a prominent criminal lawyer named Tom Martin, who took Lyndon in and gave him a job until he decided to go back home. After his return, he went to work on the county road gang—prob-ably a patronage job, arranged by his father. He shoveled gravel, drove a truck, pushed a wheelbarrow, and, according to Booth Mooney's book *The Lyndon Johnson Story*, "did a reasonable amount of helling around on Saturday nights." On one of those nights, he wrecked the family car. But it was re-placed with a new one the next day, and he was quickly forgiven by an in-dulgent father.

The road work, after a couple of years, bored him. As his mother told the story, Lyndon came home one cold day and announced to his parents: "I'm sick of working just with my hands and I'm ready to try working with my brain. Mother, if you and Daddy will get me in college, I'll go as soon as I can."

So he hitchhiked to Southwest Texas State Teachers College at San Marcos. There he got a job in the president's office (after a phone call from his father), worked part-time as a janitor, studied history, became a debater and won a debating prize for opposing the proposition "Resolved, that the United States should cease to protect by armed forces, capital invested in foreign countries except after a declaration of war." He also became a writer for the college newspaper. His editorials reflected the state of his political philosophy, and there was, to say the least, no apparent "populism" in his preachings. He exhorted his contemporaries to emulate Horatio Alger: "What you accom-plish in life depends almost entirely upon what you make yourself do. If you wish strongly enough to do a thing you will be willing to go through all kinds of trials to accomplish the work you have undertaken." Charles Lindbergh, in Lyndon's view, was a case study in how "pluck" conquers all: "Students, the choice is with you. Do not sigh for Lindbergh's wonderful luck, but deter-mine to emulate Lindy's glorious pluck." He wrote in other articles on the need for "getting ahead," the virtues of "thrift," "sincerity," "playing the game." A student of Johnson's early years summed it up best: "His was the temper of Poor Richard's Almanac, the spirit of McGuffey's reader. It was, above all, an essentially American spirit."

For a year after his graduation from Southwest Teachers, he taught in a public school. But that was a minor way station in his life, although in later years he made much of it. His real ambition was to get ahead. In 1931, he got his chance. Richard Kleberg, one of the millionaire owners of the huge King Ranch, ran for Congress and Lyndon's father campaigned hard for him. When Kleberg won, Sam Johnson called for the *quid pro quo*—a job for his son as Kleberg's administrative assistant in Washington. Kleberg agreed and Lyndon was on his way.

This episode was symbolic of Lyndon Johnson's political life. For all his talk in college about self-reliance, pluck, grit, and triumphs over adversity, Lyndon invariably relied on political influence and political connections in advancing his own career. As Horace Busby said after his death: "He had always had a mentor. He always learned from the top. He dealt exclusively with men of power and influence."

Kleberg took him to Washington. Franklin Roosevelt blessed him with patronage. Sam Rayburn and Richard Russell promoted his congressional ambitions. John Kennedy made it possible for him to become President. His strength and his greatness lay in his ability to use men and to capitalize on his opportunities. But it remains true—and is central to an understanding of Lyndon Johnson—that at every crucial step in his life he had powerful sponsors in the established order.

Political Washington in 1931 was a grander stage than Johnson had known before. Still, in many ways, it retained the character of a Southern town. The federal establishment was not the Leviathan it was to become in later years. There were only forty-three people on the White House staff and only 800 in the headquarters of the State Department. It was a milieu in which a young, ambitious Texan could be comfortable and practice the small-town politics he had learned back home.

He was twenty-three when he arrived, gifted even then with the capacity to fit his ambitions to his opportunities. In college he had politicked his way into campus offices. In Washington he politicked in the only arena available—the club of congressional assistants known as the Little Congress. He was elected "Speaker" of the organization after a carefully calculated campaign, and he profited from it. "Though the Little Congress had no official functions," his brother Sam later wrote,

it gave my live-wire brother an opportunity to meet and become intimate friends with congressional secretaries from all over the country. And in the course of their leisurely socializing, he learned an awful lot about their bosses, about their strengths and weaknesses, their pet legislative projects, their ties with other congressmen, and their real political inclinations as opposed to their public views. He knew firsthand about Congressman So-and-So's troubles with a labor union back in Denver and how he had barely squeezed through with only 312 votes in the last election; about Senator Smith's worries with an up-and-coming governor who would challenge him in the next election; that Congressman Jones drank too much but never failed to show up for a vote on farm subsidies. . . . Fascinated with anything that concerned Congress and the people who make it run, he absorbed all that information because he had . . . the kind of mental computer that never rejects any data, however irrelevant it may seem at the moment of input . . . Apart

job, became heavily involved in the social life of political Washington, and established himself firmly in the power structure of the city.

Philosophically he had arrived at that hybrid, nonideological stance that he was to retain throughout his life and which he once described better than any of his biographers:

"I am a free man, an American, a United States Senator, and a Democrat, in that order. I am also a liberal, a conservative, a Texan, a taxpayer, a rancher, a businessman, a consumer, a parent, a voter, and not as young as I used to be nor as old as I expect to be—and I am all these things in no fixed order."

He was a man, in short, for all factions and seasons and he came to that all-encompassing position very early in his political career.

In an address to the Texas Legislature in 1941 he summed it up:

"I come to you today as a friend of American labor. But to labor I want to say this: when you vote to strike you must think not only of your liberties but also of those superior liberties of every citizen of your country. You must think of your government and what it requires to save you and your precious rights.

"I have been the friend of business and industry. Still there are privileges superior to yours and above those of any other minority in America. Your government can call on you and you are bound to respond when it must defend you and your precious advantages.

"I have fought a long battle for the farmers. But to farmers I say: Government can call on you, too, and you must answer.

"The security of the whole country is above that of any single group—labor, capital, or farmer. When, in the scramble to save yourselves, individually, all you minorities become willing to sacrifice the whole people for yourselves, you will jump the trap of your own gallows."

This ideological neutrality served him well in Texas. He was unopposed for re-election in 1938 and 1940, and in 1941 he ran a strong race for the U.S. Senate. He lost but the loss cost him nothing. He retained his House seat and a statewide following.

A few months later the United States was at war. Within days after the attack on Pearl Harbor, Johnson entered the Navy—the first congressman to go into uniform. In some accounts of his life, this episode is recounted proudly and with some justification. Lyndon ᴠ   a patriot, a believer in America and its purposes. He believed, too, that there was a definable "national interest" at all times and undoubtedly believed that it was his duty—perhaps his privilege—to serve his country when it was at war, to set an example for the people who had elected him. From that perspective there was nothing "phony" about his willingness to enter the armed services when the war came. He was not obliged to do it. He could have remained in Congress as most of his colleagues did. He could have claimed that he had a higher duty and a larger responsibility than the mere act of putting on a uniform. Instead, he chose to enter the Navy.

But that act—like so many acts in his life—was flawed by the compromises he made. He did not resign his congressional seat. He did not enlist in the

A U.S. naval officer's photograph inscribed for a friend

armed forces to take his chances like an ordinary man. Instead, he sought the best of both worlds. He obtained—because of his political influence and his seat on the Naval Affairs Committee—an instant commission as a Lieutenant Commander in the Navy, a rank that a career officer would have spent years to achieve. He underwent none of the arduous training, none of the routine humiliations and hardships that were the lot of the average serviceman. Instead, he was assigned to an office job in San Francisco, working with the United States–New Zealand Navy Command. When he wearied of that assignment, he made a personal trip to the White House to obtain a more interesting job overseas. He got it. He was directed to go out to Australia to serve with General Douglas MacArthur for the purpose of preparing a report for President Roosevelt. That is the kind of job that only the most privileged political operators could expect. It ensured him an easy and fascinating tour at the highest levels of warfare. It protected him from real danger. It insulated him from the normal processes of military assignment and command. It guaranteed that he would not subsist on K-rations or spend his nights under fire in fox-holes or on the deck of a destroyer.

He did fly on a reconnaissance mission over New Guinea. The plane was shot at, was hit, and was forced to make an emergency landing back in Australia. For being a passenger on that flight, Johnson was awarded the nation's third highest decoration for valor—the Silver Star. It was given to him personally by MacArthur, one of the most political of American generals. The congressman, MacArthur said in his citation, "evidenced marked coolness in spite of the hazard involved . . . his gallant action enabled him to obtain and return with valuable information." Silver Stars were not ordinarily handed out for junkets of that kind. It was purely and simply a "political" decoration. Yet Johnson not only accepted it but after he became President almost always wore a Silver Star ribbon in his lapel. And in private conversation years later he often said he "knew what it was to be in combat" and would then tell the story of MacArthur pinning the medal on him for bravery.

Shortly after that incident, he decided to return to Washington to resume his seat in Congress. He had spent just seven months in the Navy. On his return he delivered a series of speeches as an expert on war. He was re-elected that year—1942—without opposition. After only five years in Congress, Lyndon's political future seemed secure. He had solid support at home, powerful friends in Congress and in the Administration. All that he lacked at that point in his life—the mid-30s—was financial security, and it was not long before that problem was solved.

Upon the death of her parents, Lady Bird came into a moderate inheritance. Her net worth in 1943 was reported as $64,332. She used part of her money that year to buy an Austin radio station, KTBC. The price was $17,500. The station's value, however, rose rapidly under the ownership of the Johnsons. The Federal Communications Commission extended the station's broadcasting hours and approved an increase in its transmitting power. At about the same time the station acquired valuable affiliation with CBS. By 1951 the Johnsons' Texas Broadcasting Corporation reported a net worth of $488,116 and an operating profit that year of $57,983. By the time Johnson reached the White House in 1963, he had acquired a television franchise from the FCC and had bought other broadcasting properties. His company's market value was then estimated at more than $7 million and the operating profits were estimated at $500,000 a year. These profits over the years enabled the Johnsons to acquire large landholdings as well as substantial blocks of bank stock. His political success, in short, was no barrier to his financial success; it was often argued, in fact, that the one followed the other.

However that may be, Lyndon Johnson at the age of thirty-five was somebody. That is a time in life when many if not most men are still wondering who they are, where they are going, what they want to be. Johnson, so far as we know, had none of those self-doubts. Politics was his life, and there was no question that he was good at it or that his future would not end in obscurity in Washington. Roosevelt doted on him, used him as a political agent and negotiator, and once said to friends in a half-joking way: "That's the kind of man I could have been if I hadn't had a Harvard education." He was intimate with the brightest and most influential men around Roosevelt, was respected by his congressional colleagues and the Texas political establishment, was popular in Washington social circles, and was growing all the time in his understanding of power and its uses.

Yet, strangely, the early Lyndon Johnson in those New Deal days is but a dim memory to many of the congressmen he served with then. He was known as Roosevelt's man, a man who ran private political errands for the President, a comer, an operator. But his own powerful personality was sublimated to that of his powerful "chief." The LBJ of colorful Washington legend would come later; then, in the Roosevelt era, Lyndon lived more in the shadows than on the center stage.

A cynic could suggest that Lyndon's relationship with FDR was another example of calculated political opportunism, a classic case of a young man on the make. But it was much more than that. On the soft spring day in 1945 when Franklin Roosevelt died, no one responded to the shock more personally than Lyndon Johnson of Texas.

Lyndon's friend, William S. White, then a reporter for the *New York Times*, found young Congressman Johnson standing in a gloomy Capitol corridor with tears in his eyes. For once, he seemed tired and withdrawn. As White reported it in the *Times*:

"He was like a daddy to me, always," Lyndon said, in his grief. "He always talked to me just that way. He was the one person I ever knew—anywhere—who was never afraid.

"Whatever you talked to him about, whatever you asked him for, like projects for your district, there was just one way to figure it with him. I know some of them called it demagoguery; they can call it anything they want, but you can be damn sure that the only test he had was this: Was it good for the folks? They called the President a dictator and some of us they called 'yes' men. Sure, I yessed him plenty of times—because I thought he was right—and I'm not sorry for a single 'yes' I ever gave. I have seen the President in all kinds of moods—at breakfast, at lunch, at dinner—and never once in my five terms did he ever ask me to vote a certain way, or even suggest it. And when I voted against him—as I have plenty of times—he never said a word.

"I don't know that I'd ever have come to Congress if it hadn't been for him. But I do know that I got my first desire for public office because of him—and so did thousands of other men all over this country."

And then his emotions took over. "God. God, how he could take it for us all."

Franklin Roosevelt remained Lyndon Johnson's hero until his own death. His passing was a political loss for Johnson, too. With the changing of the guard at the White House, he no longer had the intimate relationship to the presidency he had enjoyed during his first years in Washington. But by that time he no longer needed to be a White House protégé. He was a figure of substance in his own right, as he showed in 1948 when he ran for the Senate in Texas and won (by eighty-seven votes) in a bitterly contested race.

His emergence as a national political figure and as one of the great legislative leaders in American congressional history quickly followed. He entered upon this role with a great wisdom about power and with a surpassing understanding of government. In all the years that had gone before he had been learning, perhaps unconsciously at times, how men were motivated, how they could be made to respond, how bureaucracies reacted to pressure and blandishment, how ideas and measures and men were bought and sold. His brother commented on this learning process and revealed, at the same time, an attitude toward "the Kennedys" that Lyndon, deep down, always shared: "That's what the later New Frontiersmen—that fancy-talking bunch of young amateurs who helplessly tried to get things moving for President Kennedy—never knew. They didn't understand a damned thing about the government."

Paul Healy of the *New York Daily News*, writing in the *Saturday Evening Post* in 1951, touched on another quality that was central to Johnson's success in the Senate: he was single-minded, a one-dimensional man. "He is entirely preoccupied with the science of politics," Healy wrote. "He refused to be trapped into thinking about or discussing sports, literature, the stage, the movies, or anything else in the world of recreation." There was no time in his life for books, for abstract speculations or leisurely socializing. Politics was his work and work was his life. He recognized, with a certain regret at times, that he was not a "well-rounded" man. He would speak with pride of his mother's literary interests, or his wife's ability to enjoy novels and "culture." Then, as later, he would refer sardonically—but with real envy—to the "Ivy Leaguers" who (like John Kennedy) were admired for their "style" and "taste." He had no time for that.

The story is told that Lyndon's father once admonished him that he didn't belong in politics unless he could walk into a roomful of men and know at once who was for him and who was against him. To a considerable extent he had that talent. Evans and Novak in their book *Lyndon B. Johnson: The Exercise of Power* described a meeting in 1957 between Johnson and the historian, Arthur M. Schlesinger, Jr. Johnson gave Schlesinger what came to be known as "The Treatment," a long lecture on the nature of leadership. "The Treatment," Evans and Novak wrote,

began immediately: a brilliant, capsule characterization of every Democratic senator: his strengths and failings, where he fitted into the political spectrum; how far he could be pushed, how far pulled; his hates, his loves. And who (he asked Schlesinger) must oversee all these prima donnas, put them to work, knit them together, know when to tickle one's vanity, inquire of that one's health, remember this one's five o'clock nip of Scotch, that one's nagging wife? Who must find the hidden legislative path between the South and the North, the public power men and the private power men, the farmers' men and the unions' men, the bomber-boys and the peace-lovers, the egg-heads and the fatheads? Nobody but Lyndon Johnson.

Imagine a football team (Johnson hurried on) and I'm the coach, and I'm also the quarterback. I have to call the signals, and I have to center the ball, run the ball, pass the ball. I'm the blocker (he rose out of his chair and threw an imaginary block). I'm the tackler (he crouched and tackled). I'm the passer (he heaved a mighty pass). I have to catch the pass (he reached and caught the pass). Schlesinger was sitting on the edge of his chair, both fascinated and amused. Here was a view of the Senate he had never seen before.

Other men were equally fascinated by his style. J. William Fulbright of Arkansas, who was to become a thorn in his side over Vietnam years later, described Johnson in those years: "He made the Senate function better than anyone. He pushed things around; he got things done. He was a hell of an operator . . . He was as dedicated to the practice of politics as any man I have ever seen. It was remarkable the attention he used to give to every bill—big and little—small and unimportant as they may be."

A presidential hopeful on the stump in 1956

Recovering from a heart attack in 1955

Majority Leader of the Senate

Johnson's shrewdness in judging men, his drive to succeed, his understanding of the uses of power and patronage and his understanding of the governmental process itself were all factors in his remarkable career as a legislative leader. But they do not, in themselves, explain how he came to dominate the Senate and its business after becoming the Democratic leader in 1954. The true explanation lies in those qualities of character and personality that made him, for all his defects, a big man.

One of those qualities was self-discipline, and in that respect he lived up to the Horatio Alger ideal that had intrigued him as a young man. He disciplined himself to work. It was self-discipline that kept his passions in check, that gave him intellectual flexibility, that enabled him to remain detached from the great ideological conflicts that divided his colleagues in the Senate. He applied discipline to his personal behavior and kept in his desk on the Senate floor a set of rules for winning friends and influencing people:

1. Learn to remember names. Inefficiency at this point may indicate that your interest is not sufficiently outgoing.
2. Be a comfortable person so there is no strain in being with you. Be an old-shoe, old-hat kind of individual.
3. Acquire the quality of relaxed easy-going so that things do not ruffle you.
4. Don't be egotistical. Guard against the impression that you know it all.
5. Cultivate the quality of being interesting so people will get something of value from their association with you.
6. Study to get the "scratchy" elements out of your personality, even those of which you may be unconscious.
7. Sincerely attempt to heal, on an honest Christian basis, every misunderstanding you have had or now have. Drain off your grievances.
8. Practice liking people until you learn to do so genuinely.
9. Never miss an opportunity to say a word of congratulation upon anyone's achievement or express sympathy in sorrow or disappointment.
10. Give spiritual strength to people and they will give genuine affection to you.

It is easy to snicker at this Dale Carnegie approach to human relations. But the truth is that human relations were decisive in his ability to lead the Senate. He could not order a senator to vote this way or that; he could not decree legislative compromises. His only real power was the power of persuasion and that power rested on his relationships to his peers. It took enormous self-discipline to "like" or seem to "like" many of his colleagues, to control his own powerful emotions, to keep his large ego in check, to "drain off" his grievances. But he managed it, just as he was able to manage his frustrated ambitions and turbulent feelings in the years he spent as Vice-President.

A second quality that set him apart in the Senate was his utter dedication to the concept of the "national interest." It is, in a sense, an arrogant or elitist concept because it assumes that out of the interplay of ideas and desires in the minds of a handful of powerful men in Washington, the "public good" can be defined. This concept came to be called "consensus politics" during Johnson's years of leadership in the Senate, and he was criticized for it on grounds that the consensus he achieved was too narrow, that it failed to reflect those "powerless" elements in American life. However, it was a far broader concept than most public men brought to their tasks and it was fundamental to his capacity to lead. He talked about it in 1960 in these terms:

"There are different viewpoints and different emphases [in the Senate] on nearly every matter. There are 50 different States with different backgrounds, different environments, different geographical and economic interests.

"In my party we have Harry Byrd and Wayne Morse, Dick Russell and Hubert Humphrey, Jim Eastland and Paul Douglas, Bill Proxmire and Strom Thurmond—all of them Democrats, all of them sent by sovereign states to speak for their states. Now, those men don't always see everything alike.

"I have one yardstick that I try to measure things by: is this in the national interest? Is this what I believe is best for my country? And, if it is, then we outline it to these fellows of various complexions—and that includes Republicans, Dirksen and Javits, Senator Case of New Jersey and Senator Dworshak of Idaho. They have their differences. The thing you must understand is that no man comes to the Senate on a platform of doing what is wrong. They will come determined to do what is right. The difficulty is finding an area of agreement where the viewpoint of a Dworshak of Idaho can be blended with a Case of New Jersey—because the commuter problem in New Jersey is quite different from what it is in Idaho—or the problem of Thurmond of South Carolina and the problem of Douglas of Illinois can be brought to some accord."

Johnson knew all this, as a puppeteer knows his dolls. And out of this profound knowledge he did bring the Cases and Dworshaks, the Humphreys and Russells together. The inevitable result in the major legislation of the Johnson years was compromise, conciliation, and accommodation. Civil rights legislation was stronger than the Southerners wished, and weaker than the Northerners demanded. McCarthy was censured, less severely than the Left hoped and more sharply than the Right wanted. "Bipartisan" foreign policies were adopted that were acceptable to a Republican chief executive and to the Democrats who would run for the presidency in 1960.

He was no philosopher in those years; he believed in doing what was possible, not in tilting at windmills or "making an issue." One of his assistants in the Senate was Harry McPherson, a brilliant young Texas liberal who anguished and bled over injustice. He came to Johnson one day to urge him to push through a repealer of the loyalty oath that was part of the National Defense Education Act. "He wheeled on me," McPherson wrote, "and leaning over until we were nose to nose, said, 'No, sir. I'm not going to do it. You liberals want me to get the Democratic party into a national debate: "Resolved: That the Communist party is good for the United States," with the Democrats taking the affirmative. I'm not going to do it.'" McPherson was disgusted but years later was uncertain whether, in that time and place, Johnson had not been right.

For such things, Johnson was blamed as much as praised. The epithet "compromiser" was hung on him by the liberals in his own party; the ADA repeatedly denounced him. Beyond that, he was regarded widely as a "wheeler-

Old friends gather in Texas: Lyndon, Harry Truman,

"Texas Jack" Garner, Sam Rayburn

dealer" and a con man because of his success at achieving "consensus." He could, as McPherson has said, "teach it round or flat, but the important thing was, he taught it." This brought him real power and real respect, if not real affection in the Senate. Because of Johnson the Senate functioned and the Democrats he led became a credible and effective force in the governance of the nation despite the presence of a Republican in the White House. But to most Americans he remained, as Tom Wicker has written, " 'just a politician' and a Southern politician at that."

It was this image, as much as anything, that barred him from serious consideration for his party's presidential nomination in 1960. And it was this image that haunted and angered and frustrated him until the day he died.

With the Kennedys in Los Angeles and Washington

President: Rise

By the spring of 1964, Lyndon Johnson was nearing the pinnacle of public acclaim. He had been President for only a few months, but the entire country was applauding his performance. He had moved confidently, with assurance, conviction, and skill, as he presided over a united America. The media was entranced by him. The intellectuals were saying he could be another Roosevelt. His old political enemies were disarmed, his old allies ecstatic. Early that April the Gallup Poll found that 77 per cent of the American people regarded him favorably, as against only 6 per cent who viewed him negatively. While the tragedy of John Kennedy's assassination was still fresh in the national consciousness, there was an almost universal belief—a "consensus," in Lyndon's favorite term—that in choosing Johnson as Vice-President Kennedy had chosen well. America was in strong and able hands.

To the country at large, and to most of those who saw him privately, Lyndon was projecting a picture of exuberant leadership. Watching him, or listening to him talk, it seemed inconceivable to think of him as a man riddled with self-doubts and torn with insecurities. But he was, even then, even in those most placid and successful days of his presidency. Occasionally, in a rare moment of private revelation, he let down the veil and exposed his deep misgivings and uncertainties.

One night that April provided a clear picture of the public—and euphoric—Lyndon as opposed to the private—and darker. Max Freedman, a newspaper columnist, had invited a number of editors attending the annual meeting of the American Society of Newspaper Editors to his home in Georgetown for late-night drinks and conversation. Soon after they had gathered in Freedman's handsome living room a surprise guest arrived—the President of the United States.

Lyndon was ebullient. The assembled editors—many of whom had never met him or been with him personally before, many of whom knew him only in terms of LBJ stereotypes and labels—were entranced. Lyndon's conversation soared. He regaled them with stories. He impressed them with the depth and breadth of his political knowledge and understanding. He mimicked famous politicians; he described the strengths and weaknesses of the great men of the Senate; he talked about power and its uses. He speculated about the vice presidency and who might run with him that fall. Hubert Humphrey, who was present that night, hung on the President's every word while Lyndon, as one of the guests recalled, "played Hubert on a pole like a bait with trout." Lyndon mentioned this man and that as a "strong" candidate and possible nominee (Eugene McCarthy and Tom Dodd among others) but never mentioned Humphrey's name.

At one point while they were all seated around the dining table, Eugene Patterson of the *Atlanta Constitution* started to introduce himself. "Mr. President, I'm Gene Patterson . . . " But Lyndon waved off the introduction, leaned forward to stare intently into Patterson's eyes, and said, "I know who you are. And I'm going to appoint you to my Civil Rights Commission. What do you think about that?"

"Mr. President, I'm flabbergasted," Patterson replied.

"Do you accept? Do you accept?" Johnson demanded.

Lyndon kept the conversation going. He was holding court before a captive, but delighted, audience. "He was so exuberant, so high," one of those present later recalled, "that some of us wondered about his mental stability."

Finally, at two o'clock in the morning, Lyndon decided to leave the party. He offered to drop Patterson, the fellow Southerner, off at his hotel on the way back to the White House. As the limousine glided through the darkness, the new President suddenly became morose. He bent forward, placed his head in his hands, and talked quietly and somberly of trouble he saw coming.

The Kennedy crowd and the intellectuals and the fancypants were never going to accept him as President of the United States, he said. They would never let him up, they would never give him a chance. They would cut him to pieces because of his speech, his mannerisms, his Southern origins. It was inevitable, he said, and no matter what he accomplished in the days and years to come, he never would be appreciated by the "Eastern crowd." They were mad that he was in the office, and they were going to get him one way or the other. Just watch. He knew his education would never qualify him in the eyes of the Ivy League; knew that his backwoods accent would gain him the nickname "Cornpone" in the smart Georgetown salons; knew the liberal redhots would never trust his background; knew most of his fellow Southerners would never forgive his demands for black rights and knew many blacks would never fully trust him for being Southern. He could read the trouble coming.

"You just wait," he said, "and see what happens when I put one foot wrong."

He had not, at that stage, made a wrong move. His first address to Congress, five days after the assassination in November, had been a memorable declaration that moved many of those in the House chamber to tears. But it was more than an eloquent address. It was, as Tom Wicker of the *New York Times* said, "exactly the right statement, delivered in exactly the right tone." Lyndon Johnson's theme was unity—national unity—and his appeal was to all Americans to move forward and transform a moment of national mourning into a national affirmation of principles and purpose.

"We will serve all of the nation—not one section or one sector or one group —but all Americans," he said. "These are the United States—a united people with a united purpose. Our American unity does not depend upon unanimity. We have differences. But now, as in the past, we can derive from these differences strength, not weakness; wisdom, not despair. Both as a people and a government, we can unite upon a program, a program which is wise, just, enlightened, and constructive."

What gave his address such force was not his style nor his manner of delivery but the unique aspects of his message. Here he was, the first Southerner to become President since Woodrow Wilson, speaking in the unmistakable accents of the Old Confederacy, saying with slow and immensely dramatic effect:

"No memorial oration or eulogy could more eloquently honor President Kennedy's memory than the earliest possible passage of the civil rights bill for which he fought."

Then, after a storm of applause: "We have talked long enough in this country about equal rights. We have talked for one hundred years or more. It is time now to write the next chapter—and to write it in the books of law."

It was a daring, a stunning example of leadership. In the days and weeks that followed, he maintained the sure and confident public touch: in his speech before the United Nations General Assembly when he called for an end to the Cold War "once and for all"; in his first State of the Union Message when he declared an "unconditional war on poverty"; in his offer to join the Soviet Union in East-West negotiations on disarmament; in his special message to Congress outlining plans for a billion-dollar attack on the problems of poverty; in his settling of the 4½-year-old work rules dispute avoiding a national railway strike. (The railroad dispute offered another example of the LBJ flavor. When he had the railroad men at the White House, as he privately told Carroll Kilpatrick of the *Washington Post*, one of them came up and said, "Mr. President, I'm just a country boy . . . " Lyndon quickly broke in to say: "Hold on there. Wait a minute. When anyone approaches me that way I know I'm going to lose my wallet." But, he continued with relish, "the fellow said he just wanted to say he agreed with me.")

Soon, that spring, he was going to the country to spell out the phrase that will always be associated with his presidency: America must move "upward to the Great Society."

Yet for all his assurance in public, for all his deftness in political maneuver and leadership, Lyndon was also privately displaying in those months the same kinds of doubts and insecurities he revealed to Gene Patterson on that night-time ride back to the White House.

His need for company and his inability to be alone: the night, just twenty-four hours after the assassination, when he returned to his home, "The Elms," and asked his aide Horace Busby to stay with him in the bedroom until he went to sleep. A half-hour after the lights had been turned off, Busby tiptoed quietly around the bed toward the door. "Buz," the voice came from the darkness. "Buz, is that you?" Yes, it was. "Buz, I'm not asleep yet." Busby returned to his chair, waited again until he was certain the President was asleep, and again got up to leave. "Buz, are you still there?" the voice called out. Once more Busby returned to his vigil. This time he waited a full hour before he could leave.

His hints that he was troubled: the time, in early April, when he strolled around the White House grounds for an hour with Ben Bradlee and Chalmers M. Roberts of the *Washington Post*, as Roberts recounts in his book *First Rough Draft*, talking all the time. He said that he slept at most only six hours and that he "sometimes wakes up thinking about problems" (though he added that he "always goes right back to sleep").

His desire to attract, and appeal to, the "best minds," but his wariness at ever being truly accepted by them, his sense that they would turn on him in the end, and his feeling, from the beginning, that his time in the White House was limited: telling Eric F. Goldman, the historian, in the Oval Office only eight days after the assassination, that he needed outside advice on goals and specific programs for his Administration but insisting that the undertaking be kept in utmost secrecy. "You know how I came to be in this room," Lyndon said. "I don't know how long I will be here. As long as I am the President, I have one resolve. Before I leave, I am determined to do things that will make opportunities better for ordinary Americans, and peace in the world more secure. But I badly need help—I badly need it. And I especially want the help of the best minds in the country."

And always, overshadowing everything else, his belief that try though he would he never could escape the Kennedy shadow and Kennedy legend. He was trapped by the Kennedy past—the Kennedy men, the Kennedy policies, the Kennedy aura, the Kennedy promise—and the Kennedy future, the restoration exemplified in those early months by that tortured "shell of a man," Robert Kennedy.

It was not, as Lyndon's critics say, a case of Kennedy paranoia. The Kennedy problem was real. The yearning for a return to the presumed lightness and elegance and nobility of purpose was being given swift and tangible expression in the Kennedy highways, the Kennedy airports, the Kennedy schools and public buildings, the Kennedy space center, the Kennedy coins, and the Kennedy eternal flame glowing on the slopes of Arlington. The Kennedy circles of Washington and the country regarded Lyndon Johnson as an imposter. He was made the butt of sneering jokes. Substantial elements of the press shared those feelings and wrote comparing him unfavorably and unflatteringly with Kennedy. It was also true that the "best people" never accepted him.

His loyal assistant Jack Valenti now says that while Lyndon was Vice President he was convinced he would never become President in his own right. Indeed, he was convinced that no Southerner in his lifetime would be elected President. Southerners, in Lyndon's mind, were hyphenated Americans, second-class citizens. The obsessions that he was to carry to his grave did not start with his accession to the presidency. As Majority Leader in the Senate he had already revealed a deep insecurity about his "image" in the East. Debating with himself, Hamlet-like, in 1960 about becoming a candidate for President he would think about these things, and they depressed him.

The "liberals" and the "intellectuals," he would say, were against him. He was right. They did despise him—because he had "compromised" too much, he had voted "Southern" for twenty years on civil rights legislation, he had supported the Taft-Hartley Labor Act and had voted to override Truman's veto of it, he was a "tool of the interests." Even his triumphs as Majority Leader were turned into another indictment. His enemies, Harry McPherson wrote, made "his primacy in the Senate seem less the result of statesmanship than of ruthlessness and the brokerage of power. . . . His reputation as a master wheeler-dealer was repugnant to those who regarded the Presidency as a moral, almost a priestly office."

Above all, though, was that cruel flaw which was, to a considerable extent, nothing more than the accident of his birth, of his upbringing, of the society from which he had sprung. He was cornpone. He talked like a Southern country boy. He acted, much of the time, like a Southern country boy. He had the mannerisms, the speech, the appetites, the gestures of a Southern country boy. He knew it (although he also knew, rightly, the depth of his own abilities and sophistication); all the people around him (including McPherson) knew it and apologized for it; all provincial Washington knew it— the journalists, the lobbyists, the agency men, "opinion-makers," all. It is impossible to believe that if he had not been what he was, he could have mastered the Senate and achieved what he had achieved. It is equally impossible to believe that he would not have been nominated in 1960 if he could have reached the liberals, the big-city bosses, the labor leaders, and the intellectuals as he reached the editors in Max Freedman's living room in April of 1964. He was overwhelming, irresistible, at times magnificent in small face-to-face gatherings. But on the public stage in New York and Chicago and San Francisco he remained a Southern country boy.

In the Senate, he had regarded John Kennedy as an attractive but inconsequential young man for whom politics was no more than a rich boy's avocation. But in the arena of national politics, before the television cameras and on the stump in Wisconsin or West Virginia or California, the roles were reversed. Kennedy was the success, the charismatic, stylish sophisticate, Johnson the bumbling Claghorn.

At Los Angeles in 1960 the truth of this difference was ground into Johnson's consciousness so deeply that he could never thereafter root it out. The ultimate humiliation came two days before Kennedy's inevitable nomination. Johnson had reluctantly become a candidate, and he challenged Kennedy to debate him in the comfortable company of the Texas delegation. Kennedy won the debate hands down and then, having won the nomination itself, offered Johnson the consolation prize—the vice presidency. Johnson had been whipped by Kennedy. He never would be able to forget it.

Nor, of course, did the Kennedys forget it. At the convention, Johnson's

55

people had charged publicly that Kennedy had Addison's disease and "would not be alive today if it were not for cortisone." And as the Democrats prepared to pick their presidential nominee, Johnson had further exacerbated the ill-feelings between the two camps by alluding to Joseph P. Kennedy, the patriarch of the Kennedy power and fortune, in terms that cast doubts on his patriotism. "I wasn't any Chamberlain-umbrella policy man. I never thought Hitler was right," he said, clearly referring to the days when Joe Kennedy had been Roosevelt's Ambassador to Britain and a defender of Chamberlain. In 1960 the Kennedys had taken Johnson's measure, beaten him, and then lifted him into executive responsibility. But if Kennedy made it possible for Johnson to become President, so Johnson's efforts in the campaign had made it possible for Kennedy to be elected President. Kennedy could not have won without Texas, and Texas, with Johnson on the ticket, stayed in the Democrat column.

The vice presidency was a painful episode in Lyndon's life, an episode we still know little about. He was guarded and withdrawn through that period. He avoided the free-wheeling private meetings with reporters at which he had always passed judgments on men and events. He left no memoirs covering that period. His brother's published reminiscences are full of bitter and angry remarks about Johnson's "miserable" treatment at the hands of President Kennedy's assistants and associates. But that account is very probably overdrawn.

What we do know is that this restless, ambitious, and enormously talented man found himself, for the first time in years, without real power. It was proposed by his successor as Majority Leader, Mike Mansfield, that Johnson should be permitted to preside over the Senate Democratic caucus after he became Vice President. The proposal was rejected out of hand by the caucus. The Democrats, as Harry McPherson later wrote, were "weary of Johnson's unrelenting management of their lives," and soon he became "just a figure around the Senate, with even less power and authority than theirs. They were courteous, but cool."

At Sam Rayburn's funeral

It was the same at the White House. Kennedy invariably treated him with courtesy and consideration—as Johnson testified to in later years. But he had no important functions, and there was a distance between Johnson and many of the men around the President. He was fully aware that Bobby Kennedy and Kenny O'Donnell had opposed his selection as Vice President and there was no easy relationship between Johnson and such men. It was true that he was invited to all the important meetings at the White House, but he sat in his chair silently on most of these occasions, creating the impression that he was sulking or antagonistic.

The press, by Johnson's lights, treated him badly. While he was in the Senate, he was able, simply through the strength of his personality, to more or less "manage" reporters and control what they wrote about him. It was an all-in-the-family relationship. But when he got on the national stage everything changed. His trips abroad inspired many critical stories and assessments, as in the case of his visit to Asia in 1961. A *Newsweek* account headlined "Yeeaaaayhoo!" described in unflattering terms the yell he let loose inside the Taj Mahal (though it was only a friendly, louder version of the attendants' demonstration of the Taj echo), described other seeming breaches of protocol and local custom, and made him appear like a country bumpkin. His impulsive decision to bring a Pakistani camel driver to the United States as his guest produced many knowing chuckles. His personal behavior was the source of considerable criticism, too—his demands for special privileges while traveling overseas, his haggling with shopkeepers, his insistence while visiting Taiwan that a military airplane be dispatched to fly in a case of Scotch whisky from Hong Kong.

At home, he was infuriated by stories speculating on the possibility that he would be dumped from the ticket in 1964 and infuriated too by the often-quoted question going around Washington in those days: "Whatever happened to Lyndon Johnson?"

Theodore White has written of that period:

Chafing in inaction when his nature yearned to act, conscious of indignities real and imagined, Johnson went through three years of slow burn, ceremonial formalities and international junketeering. It is to his credit that he was able to forgive and forget and later use so many of the men who had, in his opinion, so abused him.

Greetings in India

*The life
and times
of a Veep*

*A camel driver
comes to town*

Performing on the diamond and politicking in Texas, November 22, 1963

In the White House, Lyndon Johnson attempted to use everyone from both the Kennedy days and his own staff. He also dealt, as he had over the years, with a network of friends, intimates, and counselors both in and out of government. His manner of operating was not surprising to anyone who had followed his long career. Lyndon, in the old and accurate definition, was not a Southern politician nor a national politician, but a Washington politician. His success was never based on the brand of personal politics that moves the masses. He was a negotiator whose gifts of persuasion moved small collections of powerful men to adopt a common course of action. He dealt with law-makers, lobbyists, men of wealth, bureaucrats. His political theory and his principle of governance was that political power in America is closely held, that great decisions are not made by popular referendum but in the private interplay of what Wright Mills called "the power elite." The system, he believed, operated on *quid pro quos*. It was a principle that served him well in Congress, and it was the central principle he took with him to the White House.

No one can say with any assurance what his own dreams were for his presidency. At times, he gave the impression that his only desire was to carry on the work begun under Kennedy—and, earlier, Truman and Roosevelt. But in 1964 Lyndon, whose ego always was as large as the man himself, also clearly was laying the foundation for a great monument, a temple that in time perhaps would surpass what Roosevelt and all the others had built. *If* he succeeded, *if* his Great Society became more than rhetoric and promise, the monument would bear the lasting imprimatur of Lyndon Baines Johnson of Texas.

We will never know how deeply Johnson was wracked by self-doubt in those first days in office, how profound were his feelings of inadequacy and fear, how much the contrast between himself and Kennedy haunted him. We do know that from the beginning he was greatly concerned, if not obsessed, with the *appearance* of his presidency and with his own image in the world. In one of his first broadcasts to the nation—a Thanksgiving Day address on November 28, 1963—he declared:

"Let all who speak and all who teach and all who preach and all who publish and all who broadcast and all who read or listen—let them reflect upon their responsibilities to bind our wounds, to heal our sores, to make our society well and whole for the tasks ahead of us."

That statement was subject to two interpretations. It was, on its face, an unexceptionable and necessary appeal for unity, understanding, and help. But one could also read into it a very personal appeal to the media to put aside preconceptions about this man from Texas, to avoid invidious comparisons with the fallen Prince of Camelot, to mute the criticisms and harsh judgments that might be made of a new President who, in Johnson's own words, was perceived as a man without "style or experience."

In the weeks that followed it became even more difficult to decide what Johnson was really after. Was he selflessly concerned with the problems of continuity and governance in a time of tragedy? Or was he primarily concerned with his own ego and his own insecurities? They were questions that intrigued all of us in the news business as he began in December a lavish and

unprecedented courtship of the press. He made himself available for private interviews to more than forty editors and correspondents. He set up long luncheon meetings with delegations from the Associated Press, United Press International, *Time*, *Life*, *Newsweek*, the *Saturday Evening Post*, the *New York Herald-Tribune*, the *Wall Street Journal*, and all three television networks—ABC, NBC, CBS. His luncheon with *Newsweek* editors lasted more than three hours. His session with ABC executives was preceded by a pre-lunch swim—in the nude—in the White House pool. He paid personal visits to Walter Lippmann and the *New York Times* editors in Manhattan, as if he were dealing with heads of state. While resting at his ranch in Texas at Christmastime, he sent an airplane to Dallas to pick up the *Times* columnist James Reston and Mrs. Reston to bring them down for a visit. He sent gifts to scores of Washington correspondents, delivered by White House limousines.

There were frequent press conferences and an endless stream of statements and telephone calls to the writers and broadcasters who, as one of his associates put it, "would define him and his policies" in the days and years ahead.

Throughout this period the questions constantly intruded. Was he promoting the national interest or a self-interest? This speculation was heightened on January 10, 1964, on a flight back to Washington from the Johnson ranch. The President talked for two hours to the reporters accompanying him. The drinks flowed freely and Johnson laid out in great detail his conception of a fruitful relationship with the press. Here are notes from that meeting:

He discussed his relations with the press and said he hoped to have the best relations by making himself more available to the press than ever before. . . . "If you play along with me, I'll play along with you. I'll make big men of you. If you want to play it the other way, I know how to play it both ways, too, and I know how to cut off the flow of news except in handouts."

. . . He didn't mind people poking fun at him but he doesn't like lies . . . People have called me [he said] anti-Semitic and anti-Negro but I'm the only man elected to represent all the people and I'm going to do the best possible job for all the people. I belong to all the people. He said he did not want Jack Kennedy looking down at him from heaven and saying he had picked the wrong Vice President. He praised Mrs. Kennedy and said he would do anything for her and the Kennedy family. But he said he wasn't going to build any libraries for himself, which sounded [to some reporters] like a crack at Kennedy.

This bold attempt by Johnson to strike a bargain with the White House correspondents was shocking to some of them; it sounded like bribery—or blackmail. But in time we came to recognize that this was the quintessential Johnson. The thirty years he had spent in the pit of Washington politics had convinced him that most men had their price, that most issues and principles were subject to compromise and to the persuasion of his own powerful personality in face-to-face encounters. That is what he meant when he quoted Isaiah. "Come, let us reason together."

He approached men and problems on a very personal basis, believing—almost naively, it now seems—that if only people knew him as he really was he would win them to his side. As Max Frankel of the *New York Times* wrote after his death, "He wanted everyone with him all the time and when they weren't, it broke his heart."

It seemed in that first year in the White House that nearly everyone was with him. And it seemed, too, that his very personal style of governance was suited to the age. His standing in the polls was high; throughout the year from 70 to 80 per cent of the people approved the way he was handling his job; John Kennedy had never done better. Endless delegations called on him in the White House and went away praising his name after hours of "reasoning together"—corporation presidents, labor leaders, Negroes, women, congressmen, diplomats, educators, young people, old people, bureaucrats, scientists, and artists. From every conceivable quarter, including, to top it all, the election returns in 1964, the evidence poured in that he was succeeding, that he had won a high place in the history books, that his doctrine of "consensus" was sound.

And yet, behind that towering facade of achievement, he remained troubled. The Kennedy obsession was rooted in his mind. He worked and talked compulsively as if, in his wife's words, there "would be no tomorrow." He bullied and mimicked his subordinates. He alternately fawned on and cursed the newspapers and broadcasters. Sometimes, in the months after the assassination, he would proudly wave a copy of a poll that proved his popularity and acceptance by the people and would then, unaccountably, say, "I don't care if I'm elected."

These signs of Johnson's inner turmoil and irritability began to emerge very early in his first months as President. Time after time he would say that Kennedy was "looking down on me from heaven" and in the next breath would speak slightingly of Kennedy's inability to deal with Congress. On a trip to Texas in early 1964 he spoke contemptuously of his press secretary, George Reedy, who, he said, "carries more useless information around in his head than any man I ever knew. You can ask him about oatmeal and he will talk for hours." A few weeks later he complained that reporters were unkind to Reedy, "picking at him, acting like he was a gladiator in an arena . . . George knows a lot more than Pierre [Salinger]. George knows what he's talking about. Pierre just bulled it through. He announced a lot of things I never heard of." His strong and ambivalent feelings about the press began to surface, too. He would tell reporters privately that he wanted them to be "big men"—with his help. And he would then single out an errant reporter as a "piss ant" or an "ingrate."

He was especially sensitive to suggestions that he was unschooled in foreign affairs. When the *Washington Post* and the *Times* questioned his handling of the Panamanian difficulties at the beginning of the year, he accused the papers of trying to negotiate with the Panamanians and run American foreign policy. He had served on the Armed Services Committee in Congress, he would say, and knew something about the real world. He was "not one of those fellows from the Ivy League who pressed for a foreign affairs post and talked a lot about foreign affairs." But he knew the subject: "They say Kennedy knew about foreign policy and I don't. I was up there participating in all the Ike decisions—Lebanon, Korea . . . I appointed Kennedy to the Foreign Relations Committee and he only attended a few meetings. They say he called the fifth desk officer [in the State Department] about things; I call Rusk." He talked gleefully one day about a minor comment he had made at a press conference: "I did it just to stick it up the *Washington Post's* ass until they choked . . . "

On April 15, he invited nine *Post* editors and writers to lunch at the White House. In a memorandum later that day, Karl Meyer, who was then on the *Post's* editorial staff, wrote:

He is indeed thin-skinned and throughout [the lunch] he dropped heckling asides about press criticism. He says he cannot do anything innocent without getting into trouble. "When I see a friend on the street, I say hello—that's a terrible thing." When he goes out on the balcony, he gets ridiculed. When he shows friends around the farm, he gets in more trouble.

He simply does not seem to have the seventh sense of a JFK in anticipating how what he does will look in print. He spoke at one point of his statement on the railroad strike in which he said he was trying to be hopeful without raising expectations that everything was solved. To his chagrin, his expression and intonation were not interpreted correctly—the New York Times said things were going bad, another paper said everything was dandy. He seems constantly surprised that the President is news, and that whatever he does will be subject to relentless and often misinformed comment.

He seldom smiles. His expression was grim throughout much of the lunch and he seemed to stare ahead in detached contemplation of mortal follies. The easy amenities don't come smoothly and there is something labored about his effort at charm. But his ears are sharp and he is enormously attentive and observant. I had the feeling of a good man who wants to do a good job but who is terribly self-conscious about being a Texan and a Southerner. After five months, he just can't relax. And understatement is a language not spoken in the White House any more.

Later, Meyer added a footnote:

I failed to catch at all the President's bold and even shameless use of his office and residence to beguile visitors—his passing out of White House match books in the same way he used to pass out ball point pens, his obvious delight in the push-button device next to his bed that raised and closed windows on a clockwork schedule, his practiced spiel in leading the tour through rooms that were once the inaccessible sanctuary of the President. . . . [He is] a bold, resourceful and big man who is utterly uninhibited by Eastern decorum and official pomposity in making precisely the impression he wants. He is the living fulfillment of Harold Laski's prescription for a successful American President—a very average man with far greater than average abilities.

At that luncheon and at similar gatherings during 1964, Johnson was extremely open in his discussions of both foreign and domestic policies and politics. He anticipated the nomination of Barry Goldwater by the Republicans, supremely confident that Goldwater would be badly beaten, and invariably had polls to support his optimism. He was confident, too, that the Senate filibuster would be broken and that Congress would pass his civil rights bill striking down discrimination in voting, public accommodations, and other areas of life. There was no doubt that he felt deeply about that bill. He had talked about it with Harry McPherson the year before. McPherson's book A Political Education includes Lyndon's description of the indignities suffered by his own cook:

"She and her husband [Johnson said] had driven my car down through Alabama and Mississippi and Louisiana on their way to the ranch. And when they got hungry what would they do? Here were these two educated black people, driving the car of the Vice President of the United States down through the South, and when they wanted to eat they had to stop at one of those country grocery stores and buy 'em some beans and Vienna sausage. And when they had to go, they would go by the side of the road. Two people who worked for the Vice President of the United States peeing in a ditch. I said, that's not right. It ought not to be that way. One of them [Southern senators] looked at me and then down at his shoes and stammered out, 'Well, Lyndon, our people will need a lot of time to make these changes' or something like that. This bill ought to pass, but there's not a chance."

When he returned to this subject in 1964, confident at last the bill would pass, he remarked that if it didn't, "I would not want to live in the kind of country we would have." Nevertheless, he worried that people would expect too much from civil rights legislation. He was worried, too, about the new militancy among black civil rights leaders and he seemed to know—intuitively —that racial troubles lay ahead, whatever Congress might do.

His sense of the national mood on civil rights, the coming election, and on other domestic affairs was, of course, vindicated by events. But he was far less prescient and understanding of what lay ahead in foreign affairs.

By the fall of 1964, he seemed, in private conversations, as confident of his abilities to manage international problems as he was confident of his abilities to manage people in Washington. He boasted to a group of reporters on October 1 that he had handled successfully every international problem that had confronted him, that he had played it cool, had bargained shrewdly, and gotten his way. He referred to a problem with Brazil and needled the newsmen present about their criticisms of him, saying "All of you said I was a cornpone bumbler who couldn't feel my bottom with both hands, who came in after that shrewd, sophisticated man with style and grace and that I would lose Brazil. But we waited until the right time and moved in our stack [of bargaining chips]."

To Johnson early in the year, Vietnam was a minor problem. He was delighted with the men who were dealing with it—Robert McNamara, Dean Rusk, General Maxwell Taylor. He was proud of his restraint—"We could have been at war ten times." He repeatedly used the phrase that was to become his campaign slogan—"We're not going North [to invade] and we're not going South [to withdraw]." In September, after the incidents in the Gulf of Tonkin and the retaliatory bombing of North Vietnam, he was worried about a coup in Saigon but had not changed his mind about the proper course for the United States:

"You have heard it said we should go North; others say we should pull out. Neither is being considered. Some say we should have neutralization. We are willing to talk about that anytime anyone can guarantee the independence of South Vietnam. But no one has anything to offer along that line yet. The fourth possibility is to do what we've been doing for ten years, help them help themselves. We feel this policy, carried out by three administrations, is wisest under the circumstances. We are doing everything we can to have a stable government. . . . We know we have problems. We are not complacent. Our first duty is to be united and support the effort there."

In later years it was often charged that even while he called for peace during the campaign in 1964, Johnson was secretly laying plans for war and the direct American involvement in Vietnam that began in 1965. But nothing of that kind was ever suggested by Johnson in the private talks we were having with him through the summer. The issue of Vietnam was not uppermost in his mind—or in the minds of the reporters he was seeing. When he did discuss it, it was often in personal terms. In October he talked about sending McNamara back out to Vietnam for an inspection tour but he was concerned that "he might get killed and he's the most valuable man I've got." He was also upset at Goldwater for "calling this McNamara's war. McNamara's a professor and he's sensitive to criticism." It was at this same meeting, however, that he first speculated aloud about the possibility of a deeper U.S. involvement.

"It may very well be," he said, "that we'll have to do some of these things [bomb the North] and the Air Force people want to bomb hell out of them. [Maxwell] Taylor thinks that would just provoke all-out war. But we may have to do some messing around up there."

With the coming of winter and with the election out of the way, his concern about Vietnam increased. On December 1, walking with reporters around his ranch, he repeated the old formula of not going North or South and told about a discussion he had had with Senator Richard Russell who had "complained a lot about what was going on . . . 'All right,' Johnson said he told Russell, 'I'll order Taylor to march North tomorrow.' And Russell said, 'No, no, no.' "

A memorandum from that day also noted: "There were several attacks [by Johnson] on Senator [Wayne] Morse for wanting us to withdraw and a bitter reference to [Joseph] Alsop [the columnist who was calling for stronger measures]."

Two weeks later in his private living quarters in the White House he expanded on the subject. A memorandum from that conversation recorded it this way:

"In the past twelve months [Johnson said] the story of Vietnam has been going up and down on a chart. The governments have deteriorated . . . North Vietnam is sending a good many men South; the Viet Cong are giving us a lot of hell . . . It is the easiest thing in the world to get into a war with China—If I drop a few bombs on them I'd get action very quickly. On the other hand, if I followed 'General Morse' instead of 'General Alsop' we would get out. That would be easy but we have chosen the harder course, to help the government to help itself. . . . "

Q: Are we going to bomb up there? After a long pause, Johnson answered, "I would not want to get committed—I am not as free with words as you are." . . . He conceded that there was basis for speculation in the press that the situation is going from bad to worse. But he said that did not necessarily justify speculation that he would widen the war . . . Then he told about Senator Russell's recent visit to the LBJ ranch. "I asked him if I should drop bombs to teach the Communists a lesson. He said no, that would mean war with China. I asked him if we should then get out. He said he would like to but that would shock the whole world, adding that he hated the way the war is going. I replied: 'So do I.' "

There was still another meeting with Johnson in December. It was at Christmastime at his ranch, and the memorandum from that talk summed up his feelings about Vietnam in these words: "The President appeared to be pessimistic and frustrated and weary with the Vietnam situation."

There had been that year another frustrating problem for him. How was he to deal with Bobby Kennedy?

Lyndon Johnson's friends say he didn't really dislike Robert Kennedy, he just never trusted him. Robert Kennedy's confidantes say he didn't really dislike Lyndon, he just didn't respect him. The question is one of semantics. That they had a mutual distaste for each other and a mutual problem, of far greater import than personal feelings, is a matter of history. Indeed, it affected history.

How Lyndon resolved his "Bobby Problem" says much about the man and his presidency. Although he kept repeating throughout those early months of '64 that "continuity" was the theme and he was merely carrying on the Kennedy Administration's unfinished business, that Jack Kennedy hadn't made a mistake in choosing him for the ticket in Los Angeles—the fact is that Lyndon knew he would never be free, never be President in his own right, until he severed the Kennedy connection.

By late June or early July he had come to a final decision, and discussed it in deepest secrecy with Abe Fortas, Clark Clifford, and James Rowe. It was inevitable: Bobby must go. But how, and when? Lyndon's hand was finally forced when he learned that the arrangements committee of the Democratic National Convention was planning a 20-minute memorial film of President Kennedy—and that Jacqueline Kennedy was now saying publicly she would attend the August convention in the interest of "helping Bobby."

With these politically explosive prospects—it was quite possible the Democratic Convention, in such an emotional setting, would act on its own and pick Robert Kennedy as the vice presidential nominee whatever Lyndon's wishes—the President acted. As Eric Goldman, who was then working uneasily as the White House's "intellectual in residence," tells it:

On July 26 President Johnson called a meeting of the arrangements committee at the White House. He wanted to be brought up to date, he explained. His eye ran down the program for the opening session. Oh, that's too bad, he said, he wanted to be present for the memorial film. But with all the pressures on him, he didn't see how he could possibly get to Atlantic City [where the Democrats would convene] for the first evening. The arrangements committee got the point. It scheduled the memorial documentary after the choice of the vice presidential candidate.

With that, President Johnson could have dropped the Bobby Problem and simply gone ahead and named his man. But he felt, probably correctly, that a good chance still existed that Kennedy would be nominated from the floor of the convention. He did not want to be put in the position of crushing an RFK nomination, and he was becoming convinced that Kennedy devotees throughout the country would be less offended in the long run if he settled the matter promptly, publicly and once and for all.

The next day Johnson called Kennedy and asked him to come to the White House. Of course, Bobby said. He was planning to fly to New York on Kennedy Memorial Library business, but that could be canceled. No, the President replied, keep that date and come and see me on Wednesday, July 29.

Accounts of that meeting between Lyndon Johnson and Robert Kennedy at 1 P.M. in the White House have been told many times: how the President was seated behind his desk, all serious official business, not the more informal and casual arrangement he took with most of his private visitors; how Kennedy was ushered to a chair at his right; how Kennedy noticed that the President's tape-recorder was on and its buttons pushed down; how the President referred to written notes on his desk as he spoke; how he slowly, gradually built up to the main point: "I have concluded, for a number of reasons, that it would be inadvisable for you to be the Democratic candidate for Vice-President in this year's election"; how, at the end of their stiff encounter, Kennedy turned to the President and said, "I could have helped you, Mr. President," and the President replied, "You are going to"; how the President went on national television the next evening to announce, with no direct mention of Kennedy, he found it "inadvisable for me to recommend to the Convention [for Vice-President] any member of the Cabinet or any of those who meet regularly with the Cabinet. . . . "; and how Kennedy, a few days later, laughed and said, "I'm sorry I took so many nice fellows over the side with me."

All this was drama enough, and the source of enough ill-will to further split the already strained relations between the Kennedy and Johnson camps. But Lyndon added the last straw.

On Friday, the day following his vice-presidential–elimination TV address, he invited three senior Washington correspondents to lunch with him at the White House. In the course of some four hours with them, he gave one of the more fragrant LBJ performances. In the highest of spirits, he relaxed, expansively, and then acted out his recent encounter with Kennedy. Lyndon loved the role.

"There was a little group that felt the Attorney General [Kennedy] was God, and that disagreed with me," he told the reporters. He would show them. "Bobby was putting out vice presidential buttons. I've been getting static everywhere about Bobby. Dick Daley and people in Michigan said they didn't want [Robert] McNamara. Stevenson clubs were being reactivated in New Jersey and California." He had to take notice.

"I wrote out three days in advance what I wanted to say to him. I asked Bobby to come and see me. He said he was going out of town on Kennedy library business and did not want to come unless it was urgent. I thought he put a thermometer in my mouth. He was playing for time. I knew damn well he had to go out of town on library business. I thought he might come over before he went."

With elaborate sarcasm, he continued: "With the patience of Job, he finally came down and talked to me. I said that since San Francisco I've been thinking about the vice presidency. You have a bright future, a great name and courage, but you have not been in government very long." It was at this point that Lyndon mockingly told how he stared at Bobby, watching him intently "like a hawk watching chickens," observed him gulp, "his Adam's apple going up and down like a Yo-yo," and continued: "I have given you serious consideration but find it inadvisable to pick you."

"I said I ought not to let you run right up to the Convention," LBJ went on. "I'm big enough to tell you now. I didn't want you to tell me I should have told you earlier." He said he had cited political problems that Bobby's presence on the ticket would create in Louisiana, Mississippi, Georgia, and told him: "I can't afford to have anyone think you are doing your job with a view to being elected Vice President. You would be unhappy as hell as Vice President. You would be crazy all the time, and driving me crazy. As Vice President I worked twenty-four hours a day. It was the most difficult job I ever had. I was miserable." He paused, and went on: "Bobby said how do you plan to announce your decision. I asked how do you want it? Bobby said he'd think it over. He said 'I want to help you.'. . . Bobby asked if he resigned if I would name [Nicholas] Katzenbach. I said I don't know, Katzenbach is a good man, but why resign? There are many precedents for an attorney general campaigning." Lyndon said he asked Bobby for names of people who could help in the campaign. "I said maybe you'll use this organization yourself some day."

Lyndon made many other comments in that long private session. Referring to the columnist Rowland Evans: "Rowly Evans is a nice young man . . . but he has not been around this town long enough to advise. So I said to tell Rowly Evans to take a jump in the river and kiss my ass." Speaking of Barry Goldwater's views on foreign policy: "On this, he can't find his ass with both hands." Citing General MacArthur's advice: "Son, don't you ever get tied down in a land war in Asia." On his own military theory: "I don't believe in goosing—go for the jugular." On Dean Rusk, his Secretary of State: "Rusk is a man of general over-all wisdom. Sweetness and tolerance like my mother." On Hubert Humphrey's qualifications to be President: "That's not the only test. It's one of the considerations. Hoover was qualified, but was a flop as President. What we need is a man who understands relations with other nations and with his fellow men and will be listened to here at home. . . . He should not be a nigra-hater and should be someone who has been elected and maybe defeated once or twice. It did me good to be defeated." On relating a story Sam Rayburn told about Dean Acheson: "Acheson is a great man, but I wish he had been elected constable at least once. McNamara, Rusk, Shriver and Bobby—the greatest handicap they have is never having been elected to anything."

But though he ranged far and wide, as always, the main thrust and the greatest source of LBJ's enjoyment that day was in telling how he had disposed of the Bobby Problem.

For the short term he had. However, his handling of the affair was to have major consequences. In the way of gossipy Washington, the accounts of his conversation with the journalists quickly got back to Kennedy. The Attorney General was enraged. Several days later he saw Lyndon again and strongly protested the breach of confidence. When the President solemnly assured Kennedy he hadn't told *anyone* about their conversation, Kennedy icily replied that the President was not telling the truth. Any hope for their ever working together again had ended. They would not sit across the same table in confidence again.

In the weeks that followed, Lyndon added to his political problems by playing out one of his most extravagant public charades. He coyly kept a number of men dangling as he toyed with their vice-presidential ambitions. For all of them—Humphrey, Eugene McCarthy, Tom Dodd—it was a humiliating experience. He even maintained that he himself was not really interested in seeking the presidential nomination. It was a position he continued to state until he died. In our last, long private meeting with him, for instance, after he had left the White House, he said he had told Lady Bird Johnson that he was thinking about not running before the Democratic Convention. She talked him out of it, he said, by telling him: "It would make it seem as though you were running away. Your friends would hang their heads in shame, your enemies would dance and rejoice." And, he went on: "Besides that, she told me that if I went back to the ranch then, I might get to drinking too much."

Like so much else in Lyndon's life, this story remains an enigma.

He did, of course, go on to Atlantic City, wringing out the last possible bit of suspense over his own nomination and his final selection of Hubert Humphrey as his running mate. But even there, in what should have been his greatest moment, he was upstaged once more by the ghosts of Kennedys past and present.

What Americans remember most about the Democratic Convention of 1964 in Atlantic City is not the coronation of Lyndon Johnson, but the emotional outpouring that greeted the Kennedy memorial period. The climax came when Robert Kennedy mounted the podium and tried to speak. There was a primordial quality in the sound that rose from every corner of the convention hall. It could not be stopped, nor stilled. Through it, Robert Kennedy stood, tears in his eyes, slim and silent and pale, trying unsuccessfully to keep his own emotions in check. Finally, he spoke.

"When I think of President Kennedy, I think of what Shakespeare said in *Romeo and Juliet*:

> When he shall die,
> Take him and cut him out in little stars,
> And he will make the face of Heaven so fine
> That all the world will be in love with night
> And pay no worship to the garish sun."

Then the John F. Kennedy memorial film was shown. Thousands in the hall wept shamelessly.

In the years to come, Lyndon Johnson's only presidential campaign would be remembered mainly for the size of his victory and for the public impression he created as he took his case to the country.

The contrast between Johnson and Goldwater was, it seemed, sharp. Lyndon was the man of peace, of patience, of restraint, of a desire to continue the movement begun during the New Deal and carried on during the New Frontier. Goldwater was the intuitive, shoot-from-the-hip candidate. His philosophy, as it was understood—or misrepresented—appeared oblivious to the complexities of the 1960's. Communism was an evil; there could be no compromise with it. Atomic bombs were a weapon; they should be used. His comments seemed shocking, and extreme. When asked what he would do about Vietnam, he said blithely: "I would turn to my Joint Chiefs of Staff and say, 'Fellows, we made the decision to win. Now it's your problem.'" If elected, the Democrats warned, he would eliminate Social Security, sell TVA, return to an age of governmental *laissez-faire*, cut social programs to the bone.

There was no choice. At least, that is the way it came over to an overwhelming majority of Americans.

Later, of course, Lyndon Johnson would pay the price for these contrasts. Later, his actions and Goldwater's policies would seem to be synonymous. But then, in the heat of the campaign, and in an atmosphere still so permeated with memories of the fallen, martyred young President, the choice was, as Senator Fulbright put it, "as profound as any that has ever arisen between the two great American political parties."

Looking back on that campaign with the comfortable advantage of hindsight, there were two other important elements. One was the muted feeling, even then, that Lyndon Johnson somehow was tainted with an air of immorality. Part of this feeling stemmed from the old belief that LBJ was an operator, a Machiavellian manipulator. But it was also based on incidents that became controversial during the 1964 political year.

Bobby Baker had been Lyndon's loyal, self-effacing assistant during the Senate years. He was Lyndon's boy, who ran the errands, helped arrange the appointments—and the deals. Now, in '64, he had become a distinct political liability. The Senate Rules Committee was investigating Baker's activities, and the papers had been full of accounts of large deals Baker had worked as Secretary to the Senate Majority Leader. There were imputations of kickbacks, of pay-offs for favors, of gifts and life insurance policies. The Baker case, the Republicans were saying, was proof that the Johnson Administration was characterized by a "wheeler-dealer" atmosphere.

"I think it is going to be a very big issue," said William E. Miller, the GOP's vice-presidential nominee. "We have here an issue that goes to the integrity of our government from top to bottom."

The Baker case, like the Watergate case years later, had deeply disturbing implications. And in 1964, as in 1972, many Americans felt they really had no choice; in both elections they were voting for the lesser of two evils.

At the end of September, Woodrow Wilson's grandson spoke out publicly in an extraordinary statement, one that would be echoed in years to come by intellectuals across America. Both political parties, said the Reverend Francis B. Sayre, Jr., dean of Washington's National Episcopal Cathedral, were "completely dominated by a single man—the one, a man of dangerous ignorance and devastating uncertainty; the other, a man whose public house is splendid in its every appearance, but whose private lack of ethic must inevitably introduce termites at the very foundation."

Lyndon, Eric Goldman says, was "choleric" at Sayre's statement. And as the White House was recovering from that shock, the President was dealt another stunning blow.

Walter Jenkins, the chief of his White House staff and over the years one of the men closest to Lyndon, was arrested for homosexual activities in a pay toilet at the YMCA two blocks from the executive mansion. It was a tragic case, one that profoundly affected Lyndon Johnson personally. He had little to say about the episode in public, but privately he showed how deeply it had cut. On October 19, he called in a few White House reporters. Carroll Kilpatrick of the *Washington Post* recorded the scene: "The President was obviously deeply moved and highly emotional. As he finished, he said: 'I had a heart attack and he had another kind of attack.'"

Perhaps because of his understandable emotion, Lyndon that day added other words that were to hurt him later. He darkly mentioned, again to quote Kilpatrick, that "obviously the GOP knew about it, for it had had Jenkins under surveillance, as it also had other White House aides under surveillance." He mentioned something about "slaughters," apparently meaning character assassinations. Then he warned of retribution after the election was over.

"Don't you worry about morals in the White House," he said. "We are going to look into this whole town when this election is over."

These threats, naturally, became public throughout Washington. They added to the impression that the President was not above engaging in dirty works himself.

En route to the Atlantic City convention

In one great moment during the campaign, Lyndon showed himself at his best. He had been planning an October swing through the South, scheduled to end in New Orleans. "Maybe New Orleans is the place to make a real civil rights speech," he said to his old friend, the patrician Richard B. Russell of Georgia.

"In New Orleans?" Russell said, uncomfortably. "That's pretty strong stuff for New Orleans."

Lyndon's New Orleans speech, delivered the night of October 9 in the grand ballroom of the Jung Hotel, was an address that only a son of the South —and, in this case, only a man truly a President of all the people—could have made. It was one of his most courageous performances. Southern ties aside, these people were not his supporters. At least two-thirds of the audience ardently opposed his civil rights policies. Lyndon met them head on.

He saved his best, and boldest, for the last. He told how he came to Washington "in the dark days of the Depression as a young country kid from the poor hills of Texas," and how he would go to listen to every speech Huey Long made. "I heard them all." The South understood that message. The

South had been kept in subjugation, divided, and politically and economically powerless. Here, he became more emotional. "Now, the people that would use and destroy us first divide us. There is not any combination in this country that can take on Russell Long, Allen Ellender, Lyndon Johnson, and a few others if we are together. But if they divide us, they can make some hay. And all these years they have kept their foot on our necks by appealing to our animosities, and dividing us."

This was something his audience understood. A hush settled over the ballroom. Lyndon's strong voice filled the void. "Whatever your views are, we have a Constitution, and we have a Bill of Rights, and we have the law of the land, and two-thirds of the Democrats voted for it [referring to the bitterly contested Civil Rights Act of 1964] and three-fourths of the Republicans, and I think any man that is worthy of the high office of President is going to do the same thing."

But, he went on, his voice rising, "I am not going to let them build up the hate and try to buy my people by appealing to their prejudice."

He told a story about old Sam Rayburn going to see a certain old Southern senator, and the senator sadly remarking how the South "had been at the mercy of outside economic interests": "They exploited us. They had worked our women for 5 cents an hour, they had worked our men for a dollar a day, they had exploited our soil, they had taken everything out of the ground they could, and they had shipped it to other sections."

What a great future the South could have, the senator had said, "if we could just meet our economic problems, if we could just take a look at the resources of the South and develop them."

Wistfully, the senator told Rayburn, "Sammy, I wish I felt a little better. I would like to go back to old"—and here Lyndon said he wouldn't call the name of the Southern state. Then, pausing for effect, he hammered out the punch line:

"I would like to go back down there and make them one more Democratic speech. I just feel like I've got one in me. Poor old state, they haven't heard a real Democratic speech in thirty years. All they ever hear at election time is nigra, nigra, nigra!"

It was a speech the likes of which the South had not heard for decades, and the Southerners present that night knew it. They gave him a roaring, standing ovation that lasted for a full five minutes.

Lyndon Johnson won his great victory in November. With 61.1 percent of the popular presidential vote, he even surpassed his mentor and model, Franklin Roosevelt. In his own name and own right, he was President. The great foundation had been laid for his monument. Now, with the backing of the vast majority of the American people, he would finish the job.

One December night after the election, he called in some of his press friends for a few hours of drinks and conversation. He was asked what he thought his electoral mandate meant. Lyndon replied:

"My honest view is that the people felt they wanted to give their President a chance to have his own term, that he was entitled to a chance. Most people want to help their President, to see him be a good President. They don't love

me or hate me, and they came through the transition from Kennedy despite some worry about a new President without class or experience who might go on adventures."

He wasn't worried, he said. "The Great Society exists. It is the leader's responsibility to protect, preserve, develop, expand, and improve it."

Then Lyndon said, looking ahead to his own full term:

"We hope your 'Cornpone' President from the Deep South will have something for Congress in January."

"You're Really Rolling Up Quite A Record"

President: Fall

On a spring day in 1966 three of the nation's best known political intellectuals met for lunch at the Quo Vadis, a fashionable midtown restaurant on Manhattan's East Side. John Kenneth Galbraith, Richard Goodwin, and Arthur M. Schlesinger, Jr., all had roles in the Kennedy-Johnson Administration. All were luminaries in the Harvard–New York–Washington liberal axis. All were celebrated political pamphleteers and political speechwriters.

They talked about Vietnam that day and about Lyndon Johnson and his war policies. The war was a terrible mistake, they concluded. Its consequences were appalling: it could lead to such greater escalation that "the world might come to an end." They resolved as they left Quo Vadis to do what they could to stop the war and to stop Johnson.

That luncheon, three journalists from the *London Sunday Times* later wrote in their book *An American Melodrama: The Presidential Campaign of 1968*, "may be said to mark the moment at which Lyndon Johnson had lost not just the support but the tolerance of the American intellectual elite."

The support or tolerance of American intellectuals had been a matter of little concern or significance during most of Lyndon Johnson's lifetime. They had not shaped his education. They had not elected him to Congress. They had not made him the Majority Leader of the Senate or Vice President. Their political adventures in the 1950s had floundered, along with their candidate for the presidency, Adlai Stevenson. They had, in the main, preferred Stevenson to Kennedy in 1960 and could claim no decisive role in Johnson's nomination or election in 1964. His instinct was to regard the intellectuals with contempt or hostility or—worse—indifference, as was the case with his White House assistant Marvin Watson. When someone appealed to Watson in 1965 to persuade the President to make a conciliatory gesture toward intellectual critics, Watson's reply was classic in its simplicity: "Fuck the intellectuals."

For Johnson, however, there were problems in such easy dismissal. There was, in the first place, a highly personal problem in his posture vis-à-vis the Schlesingers, Galbraiths, and Goodwins of the world: for all his instinctive distrust and distaste for the intellectual breed, he cared what they thought. He cared deeply. They not only read books, they wrote books, and he was obsessed by his knowledge that *they* would write the histories and assessments that would help define his own place in history.

Johnson's second problem with the intellectuals was one of power. They may have been politically impotent in the 1950s, but by the mid-1960s they had developed—because of Vietnam—an important constituency. The largest element in this constituency was what Theodore White has described as the "campus proletariat." It had grown from about 1.5 million college and university students in 1940 to more than 7 million in the late '60s. They were more numerous than farmers or steelworkers or miners or the hard-hats of the construction industry. They were the children or siblings of an even larger constituency—the New Class, which Eric Goldman has defined as the Metroamericans, the educated, affluent, book-reading professionals, technicians, and managers of the high-income neighborhoods of the central cities and suburbia. This group included, as Goldman noted, the people who were dominant "in the world of books, magazines, radio and television," the people who were most sensitive to the shifting currents of thought in the intellectual class, the people who read the intellectual journals and who gave mass circulation to the political criticism the intellectuals produced.

The electoral potential held by this intellectual constituency was to shake the foundations of American politics in the primaries of 1968. Before the end of Johnson's presidency, the intellectuals would produce devastating and highly effective critiques of his foreign policy, his domestic policy and of his capacity to govern, and their constituents would shatter Lyndon's "consensus," destroy his credibility, and—in the short run, at least—destroy his reputation as well.

Johnson sensed these dangers, intuitively, from his first days in the White House. Whatever his personal tastes in men, whatever his ambivalent feelings toward the intellectual class, he believed deep down, as he told Gene Patterson in April, 1964, that "this Eastern crowd" would try to destroy him "when I put one foot wrong."

There was some paranoia and self-pity in that expectation. But it was not all paranoia, as Eric Goldman revealed to Carroll Kilpatrick of the *Post* after two years' experience in the White House. From Kilpatrick's 1966 memorandum:

From the beginning [Goldman said] the intellectuals showed "an unbreakable snobbery" about LBJ. They regarded his political skill as his greatest drawback; they assume anything he does is for political reasons. He feels that the intellectuals from the Northeast will never be for him. To him, an idea is something that tells him what to do tomorrow. He has used intellectuals more than any other President—but always to ask what he should do next. He has no interest in the intellectual process, and the intellectuals recognize this. . . . He loathes [Woodrow] Wilson because he sees him as an intellectual who failed to get Congress to support him and couldn't put his programs over. . . . The Kennedys and the intellectuals get mixed up in LBJ's mind. Goldman described LBJ's liberalism as "populism touched with Herbert Hoover." The President "deeply cares about civil rights, water problems, poverty problems," etc. but he thought his heart was not really in the problems of the cities. It was not a real part of his experience. LBJ [Goldman said] now calls [John F. Kennedy] "a little snip." He thinks LBJ is terribly insecure, something of a loser. One day Goldman told LBJ how all Democratic presidents of this century—Wilson, FDR, Harry Truman—had their work in domestic reform interrupted by wars. LBJ replied: "History shits on all of them."

. . . The tragedy of the lack of rapport between LBJ and the intellectuals is that his antagonism makes him do the opposite of what they propose.

This process of mutual and progressive disenchantment between Johnson and the people symbolized by Galbraith and Schlesinger was a complicated thing. Part of it, undoubtedly, was the President's style. Flushed with his great electoral victory in 1964 he began to appear in his moods of ebullience as a crude exhibitionist. There was, in 1965, that celebrated and much-publicized tour of his ranch with Washington correspondents. He loaded them into white Lincoln Continentals and roared down the highways at 80 miles an hour, drinking Pearl beer out of a paper cup, hugging the women correspondents, frightening the Secret Service agents. There was the occasion after his gall-bladder operation when he pulled up his shirt and posed for photographs showing off the barely healed scar. There were the times when he lifted his dogs by their ears to the dismay of humane societies all over America. One gaucherie followed another to the distaste of those who still longed for the style and grace of John Kennedy and who still regarded Lyndon as a usurper.

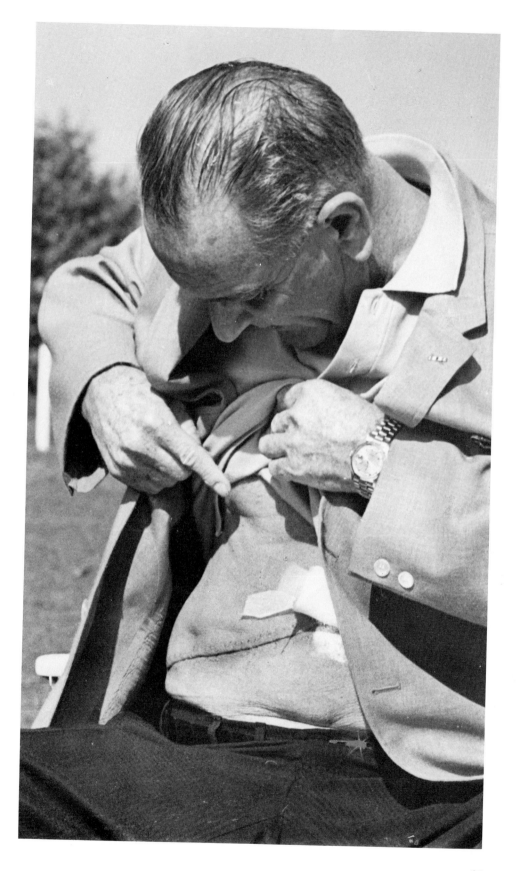

94

"Did The Music Man Say When Our Instruments And Uniforms Are Coming?"

Lyndon campaigns
for a Kennedy—
in his own style

But beyond that were the dubious foreign policy decisions made in 1965 that began, in the minds of his intellectual critics, to overshadow and corrupt all that he was accomplishing in domestic affairs. There was the intervention in the Dominican Republic, which shocked many liberals and inspired the first searching examination of his foreign policies by J. William Fulbright as Chairman of the Senate Foreign Policy Committee. Above all, there was the growing involvement in Vietnam. Early in 1965 the bombing of North Vietnam increased in intensity and in frequency. Marines were landed to defend American installations. Then came the steady commitment of troops to fight the ground war, a commitment that was not to end until more than 500,000 American men were fighting in "that dirty little war"— young men mostly, who would, before it was over, be dying at the rate of more than 300 a week.

It was not merely that the intellectuals, as Johnson feared, hated him for himself. He lost them, because of the conjunction of his personality and his policies. And in losing them, he ultimately lost the country. Not even Johnson, for all his intuition, anticipated such an outcome as he entered upon the presidency in January, 1965, in his own right.

Month after month during a President's time in office, the public opinion polls keep testing the vagaries and fickleness of the American mood. Like the stock market, a graph of a President's popularity ratings has its peaks and valleys. A crisis, a calamity, a sudden change, a surge of confidence or a tremor of fear, sometimes even a single speech, can send the statistical charts plunging upward or downward before the impersonal lines right themselves and find their proper level as they portray a President's course.

It is one of the paradoxes of Lyndon Johnson's presidency that at a time when dissent was slowly rising in the most influential circles, when actions in Santo Domingo and Saigon were sowing the seeds for graver public consequences to his national "consensus," when, indeed, the steps were being taken that entrapped America in the longest, most divisive war in its history, a war everyone had warned and counseled against, a true land war in Asia, his public opinion ratings remained at a remarkably constant and high level.

Throughout 1965, Lyndon's public approval rating as measured by the Gallup Poll never dropped below 62 per cent. Most of the time between 65 and 70 per cent of the American people viewed his performance favorably. Only slightly more than 20 per cent expressed disapproval of the way he was conducting his job as President. The reasons were not hard to find. In that period, domestic concerns were paramount. America was in the midst of the final flowering of its civil rights revolution, and the country—and the world —watched transfixed as the South's emotional drama was enacted daily on the nation's television sets and reported in its newspapers. It was Lyndon Johnson, the Southerner, whose fate it was to preside over the nation's destiny at that critical moment, and his handling of the crisis won him broad public support. It was one of his most successful periods as President.

In many respects, the conflict was inevitable. The racial revolution in the South, as exemplified first by the Supreme Court's 1954 decision striking down public school segregation and subsequently by the blacks' own militant civil rights movement in 1956, posed a threat to the very heart of the Southern—and, eventually, the national—system of separation of the races. Even Southern moderates were disturbed by the sudden changes, and by what they interpreted to be the menacing moves of the federal authorities in Washington. The conflict spread rapidly across the South, and primarily the rural South where most blacks lived. Out of this civil rights movement came a decade of turbulence and violence.

Statistics tell only part of the story. In the 10-year period from 1955 to 1965 some one thousand instances of racial violence, reprisal, and intimidation were reported. In the same period, 225 bombings occurred, many of them of churches, and more than forty persons connected with the civil rights movement in the South were murdered. The gazetteer of trouble spots grew steadily: Birmingham, Alabama, and Jacksonville, Florida; Oxford, McComb, and Philadelphia, Mississippi; Bogalusa, Louisiana, and Albany, Georgia. The Ku Klux Klan was reborn in the South and fiery crosses lighted the skies of countless Southern communities (a thousand flamed in one month alone in 1960). Hooded nightriders rode again, leaving terror and destruction in their wake. Floggings and brandings, castrations and other barbaric acts were employed as weapons of coercion. Law enforcement agencies and the bench were successfully infiltrated by the Klan, often making it impossible to bring known offenders to justice. In some communities the breakdown of law and order was total: the Klan provided the only effective force.

As the civil rights movement grew in size and strength, and as the new civil rights acts were placed on the national statute books, there was an increasingly violent reaction. Often the principal targets became white Southerners themselves, those ministers, lawyers, editors, teachers, and businessmen who were attempting to lead their region out of the past. After a series of dramatic encounters between civil rights advocates and the inheritors of the Confederate legend, all the disparate forces came together in a historical upheaval.

Ironically, that battle was fought in Selma, Alabama, the scene of the Confederacy's last stand. One hundred years later, the slumbering town in the heart of the rural "black belt" of the Deep South, a minor trading center beside the Alabama River along the Jeff Davis Highway some forty miles from the capitol of the Confederacy in Montgomery, became the scene of an emotional confrontation between black and white, old and new.

The Selma story began on January 2, 1965, when Martin Luther King called for massive street demonstrations there if blacks were not permitted to register in larger numbers. Within a month, King himself had been arrested during demonstrations. The situation in Selma, tense though it was, probably never would have become a national *cause celebre* had it not been for one factor: television. Early on the evening of March 7, a Sunday, civil rights marchers set out on the road from Selma to Montgomery to present their demands to Governor George C. Wallace and the Alabama legislators. They got as far as the Edmund Pettus Bridge over the Alabama River at the southern edge of Selma. There, they met Sheriff Jim Clark and a mounted posse. When the sheriff ordered them to turn around, they refused. The next scene was carried, electronically, into the homes of Americans everywhere. The posse rode into the marchers and, with nightsticks, bullwhips, billy clubs, cattle prods, and tear gas, left men, women, and children either beaten to the ground or fleeing for their lives.

The battle was not over; it was just beginning. Plane loads of demonstrators from throughout the country brought more recruits into Selma and the struggle in the streets became more severe. Several nights later the news from Selma was worse.

Lyndon and Lady Bird were hosting a congressional reception in the East Room of the White House when one of the President's aides brought him an urgent message. James Reeb, a white Unitarian minister from Boston, had been clubbed to death on a Selma street that night by a band of white men to the shouts of "Hey, nigger lover." The Johnsons immediately excused themselves and went upstairs to call Mrs. Reeb. As Lyndon later wrote in his book, *The Vantage Point*:

No matter what I could find to say to her, I had no answer to the one question that kept turning over in my mind: How many Jim Reebs will die before our country is truly free?

. . . . As I watched the reruns of the Selma confrontation on television, I felt a deep outrage. I believed that my feelings were shared by millions of Americans throughout the country, North and South, but I knew that it would probably not take long for these aroused emotions to melt away. It was important to move at once if we were to achieve anything permanent from this transitory mood. It was equally important that we move in the right direction.

He may have been right in thinking that the emotions were transitory and would soon "melt away." But Selma had touched a nerve and become a cause. There were mass demonstrations, rallies, and sit-ins in Paris, London, New York, Boston, San Francisco, and Washington. Soon citizens who had never participated in a demonstration before were joining hands and singing the civil rights anthem, "We Shall Overcome."

In this setting, Lyndon acted swiftly and confidently. He met with Governor Wallace at the White House, dealt with the Justice Department on the details of a historic voting rights bill, conferred with congressional leaders, and then personally wrestled with a draft of a speech he would deliver at night, live on nation-wide television, before a special session of Congress.

He was, as he wrote later, profoundly affected by the civil rights crisis. "Once again," he said, "my Southern heritage was thrown in my face. I was hurt, deeply hurt." He determined to act forcefully.

His March 15th speech before the assembled members of Congress and leaders of the American government was unforgettable.

"I speak tonight for the dignity of man and the destiny of democracy," he began. ". . . At times history and fate meet at a single time in a single place to shape a turning point in man's unending search for freedom. So it was at Lexington and Concord. So it was a century ago at Appomattox. So it was last week in Selma, Alabama."

The chamber was tense as he spoke. He speeded up his delivery.

"There is no constitutional issue here. The command of the Constitution is plain. There is no moral issue. It is wrong—deadly wrong—to deny any of your fellow Americans the right to vote in this country. There is no issue of states' rights or national rights. There is only the struggle for human rights. . . . This time, on this issue, there must be no delay, no hesitation, and no compromise with our purpose."

Selma, he said, was one of those rare times "when an issue lay bare the secret heart of America itself." And: "Even if we pass this bill, the battle will not be over. What happened in Selma is part of a far larger movement which reaches into every section and state of America. It is the effort of American Negroes to secure for themselves the full blessings of American life."

He had come to the most emotional part of his speech. Pausing, then raising his arms over his head, he said:

"Their cause must be our cause too. Because it is not just Negroes, but really it is all of us who must overcome the crippling legacy of bigotry and injustice. And," slowly, deliberately, "We . . . shall . . . overcome."

Lyndon got his voting rights act. By his action in federalizing the Alabama National Guard and ensuring the peaceful completion of the Selma-to-Montgomery march, he resolved a major American crisis. Within a few days, after a white woman from Detroit, Mrs. Viola Liuzzo, was murdered by the Ku Klux Klan on the road from Selma to Montgomery, he announced the arrest of the suspects by the FBI and again spoke out strongly, as only a Southerner most effectively could do, about the Klan:

"My father fought them many long years ago in Texas and I have fought

them all my life because I believe them to threaten the peace of every community where they exist. I shall continue to fight them because I know their loyalty is not to the United States of America but instead to a hooded society of bigots."

His performance in this period was superb. When Gallup took the next popularity rating that spring nearly seven out of every nine Americans polled said they approved of the way their President was acting. It was unfortunate, we can now see, that Americans then and later, never knew the private Lyndon. However well he was handling his public job, and however much he desired to be loved, citizens saw him only in his official capacities or as the stereotyped figure they thought him to be. Had they truly seen him they might not have loved him, but at least they would have understood, and perhaps appreciated, him better. It would have helped both the President and his country when real trauma developed later.

The days immediately following Selma provided one of those glimpses of Lyndon, the man. He flew down to the ranch, accompanied by the usual press entourage, to relax at home. There, Lyndon was at his most hospitable. He gathered the reporters around, escorting them in and out of a motorcade that took them to his boyhood home and then to his mother's bedroom where he showed off cabinets full of Lyndonia—letters to his mother, inordinately affectionate and signed "Lyndon Johnson," letters to his grandmother signed "Lyndon Baines," family pictures, marriage licenses, and other mementoes— and then on to the "Lewis place" for another tour. As he and the reporters traveled and visited, stopping and starting, clouds of dust rising in the air, Lyndon pointing to deer and to a place where he once picked up an abandoned child on a dirt road, he told story after story, hour after hour, in a monologue that lasted from front porch to front porch and through miles of presidential ranchland. Some of his stories seemed pointless; others revealed much about his own attitudes toward race, politics, and the future.

He told how a man whose shoes he once shined gave him a quarter (it was the first time he ever knew there was such a thing as a tip) when everyone else was paying a dime for a shine. How he got from Franklin Roosevelt the "Pedernales REA loan—the biggest co-op in the world both in area and power": "First time I went in to see him I got shunted out so smooth after he gave me a speech I never had a chance to talk about the Pedernales co-op, so the second time Pa Watson told me to bring photographs of dams, the chief loves photographs of dams, so I had photographs of the arches and photographs of the power lines going overhead and photographs of a few sharecropper's huts, and he looked at them and said 'Those are great arches' and 'Where's that dam?' and 'Why won't they let you have any of that power?,' and so he called over Grace Tully and told her to make the right calls and tell them to give this fella a break for me.' " How he was going to fix up that old log cabin his grandfather, Sam Johnson, built when he first came to the hill country and founded Johnson City: "It's all falling down now and I'd like to fix it up, but the man who's living in it, he's independent. Offered him $3,000 for it but he wouldn't sell, he was suspicious, thought there must have been oil or something under it, and he wouldn't take it. Going to have to go back and offer him twenty-two hundred and let him work me up to twenty-five, maybe."

He talked about cattle and football players and rednecks and then said to his guests of the press, "Now all you ladies and Doug Kiker can have a beer, the rest of you will have to wait; there'll be some coming out here a little later." (Inside 10 minutes a helicopter landed, carrying beer, on ice.) He told how he knew about Negroes and their problems from what had happened in Johnson City: "This man Winter, he was the best superintendent of a road crew. Well, he said he didn't want to take the job because his crew chiefs were all niggers, and he'd heard it wasn't good to bring niggers into Johnson City. But he was told to take it, and he did, and he had a nigger cat crew chief and nigger workers and he brought 'em all up and they camped just down on the flats by the river outside town and Winter, 'Ole Mel,' he was in the barber shop getting a shave when the town bully came up and said 'You must be the man that brought them niggers to town. You get 'em out. We don't want no niggers here,' and Mel, he said any man in town could have a job if he wanted it, but the niggers had been with him a long time and they was gonna stay. And the bully clipped him on the jaw—right here—and his head hit the metal step on the chair and knocked him cold, and they threw water on him and brought him to, and then they roped off the street. We-ll, they didn't rope it off, they just grouped around it, blocked it off—that was right down by the drug store in front of A.W.'s office—and they had a fight. Well, it lasted an hour and a half and the bully's eye was tight and so was Mel's and they were bloodied up and until—here, Paul, you hold this beer— and Mel was on top finally, and he took both hands like this on the other feller's hair and said 'Okay, the niggers stay' while the feller's head was banging on the pavement. And there never was any trouble after that in Johnson City about niggers."

He told other stories, still colloquially, but about the more serious business he had just faced in Congress and the country. How he had called in the congressional leaders before his speech on Selma, and what had happened: "John McCormack was talking to me about the voting rights speech and he said I ought to tell the Congress what I told him, that was on Friday. Now John McCormack, he's a remarkable man. If you want to get something bulled over if you get the ball inside the 10-yard line and you need a fullback to get those last few yards, John is your man. He's been underrated. He stood there and took it in the shadow of Sam Rayburn for twenty-five years. And then on Sunday, when the leaders came in they said, Mansfield, he said I ought to speak to a joint session of Congress and Dirksen he said—. Ole Ev's been wonderful. You know, I'm real worried about him. I sent a plane after him, you know, when his wife called and she was in tears. [Senator Everett Dirksen, the Republican minority leader, had been hospitalized during the Selma crisis. He died of cancer in 1969.] So I wanted to give the speech on Tuesday, but they said Monday. No, I didn't expect the speech would answer everything or stop anything."

He also told how wonderfully three of his closest aides had performed in helping him with that speech: "It was mostly three men. Of course, first it was Bill Moyers. He's in on everything, he's a remarkable young man. I think he'll be dead at forty, he takes everything so hard. And it was Horace Busby— you know, he's both objective and subjective. He can take a lot of legal language and make something out of it. And Jack Valenti. He's a genius. Comes along and he takes a paragraph of Busby and makes a sentence out of it. It gets Busby mad, but it's even better. And Dick Goodwin. He's wonderful, that boy. He can cry a little. He cries a little with me whenever I need to cry over something, and Hubert, he's another one who can cry pretty good over something. They get a lot of emotion into their work. But the speech started with Justice, only it wasn't much, it was putrid, and Buz, he whipped it into shape and then I went over it—maybe about half of it I dictated— and then Goodwin he came in and he made it sound like me. He made it sound more like me than I did. You know, that boy can do anything. There are three people the doctors said they wanted to keep an eye on: Moyers, he's had stomach trouble, and then George [Reedy], he's all heart, can't drink and can't eat now, and then Jack Valenti, the doctor said he'd never seen him so gray, and he wants me to send him away. I've tried to tell him to go, I've sent him off, but he won't go. He's wonderful to have. He's my chief of staff on Montgomery. He keeps phoning me with the reports he's getting every half hour."

Then, finally, Lyndon spoke more seriously. He was the President now, speaking of the country and race relations and his own perspective of the best way to accomplish necessary goals:

"Things are all right in Selma. I think they could have done more good marching on Washington, putting pressure on the congressmen or on me, but they have to let off steam somewhere. You have to let the cork out of the bottle. No, I don't expect trouble, I don't look for disaster. I don't think the march is going to help the situation in Alabama. I sent the provost marshal down there and his estimates of the force needed were a lot less than Governor Wallace's. He thought the Governor could have done it all with his 389 state troopers if he had a mind to.

"You know, I didn't want to make him [Wallace] look bad in public. You force a man to the wall and he can only give you one answer. But he talked good when he came up to Washington. He said he could call out the whole ten-thousand guard if he had to keep order. But then he got back to the hotheads in the Legislature down there and I don't know what happened. But I'm glad you asked that question so I could say I didn't want to question his motives. Lady Bird said I sounded like I was questioning his integrity in my statement, but I don't want to do that and try to ruin a man in public.

"It's like the man who wrestles his wife for an hour and finally pins her shoulders to the ground. As he lifts his 250 pounds up off her, he says I can lick any little hundred-pound woman in the world.

"Now, I don't want to do that, say that the President of the United States can beat any man."

Lyndon Johnson's civil rights achievements were not long unshadowed by other events. By the summer of '65, the first of the great urban riots, in Los Angeles's Watts, had begun to shatter the common cause of blacks and whites marching together. Lyndon had always feared that prospect. As early as April of 1964 he was voicing private apprehension about the future course of American race relations. People expected too much of the congressional bills, he would say, and "the young Negro leaders were showing fiery impatience." But he understood, even as he saw the trouble coming.

The riots spread across the country to such places as Detroit and Newark and New York and Washington and Atlanta. Simultaneously, the war in Vietnam was beginning to press in on the American consciousness. Lyndon's national consensus politics, we all saw—and he saw—began to be destroyed.

But in time, it seems fair to suggest even at this writing, his domestic achievements will be remembered and appreciated. He did, as Nicholas von Hoffman wrote, fight our second Civil War and carry out our second Reconstruction. And in dealings with Congress throughout 1965 he set a legislative record that is certain to endure. Bill after bill was drafted and enacted into law, acts that in the mass added up to something close to a social revolution in America. The roll-call is long and impressive: Medicare; aid to education; a four-year farm program; the Department of Housing and Urban Development; the Housing Act; a Social Security increase; the Voting Rights Act; a fair immigration law; bills improving the lot of older Americans; bills strengthening health, cancer, and stroke research; a National Crime Commission; drug controls; more mental health facilities; more medical libraries; the anti-poverty program; more aid to the arts and humanities; aid to Appalachia; highway beautification programs; clean air and water pollution control, and water desalting measures; aid to small businesses; increased community health services; steps toward arms control; juvenile delinquency programs.

All these were part of the framework of the Great Society. Some have been dismantled, or have disappeared with changing political fortunes. Others have become standard fixtures of American society—under attack, it is true, but surviving.

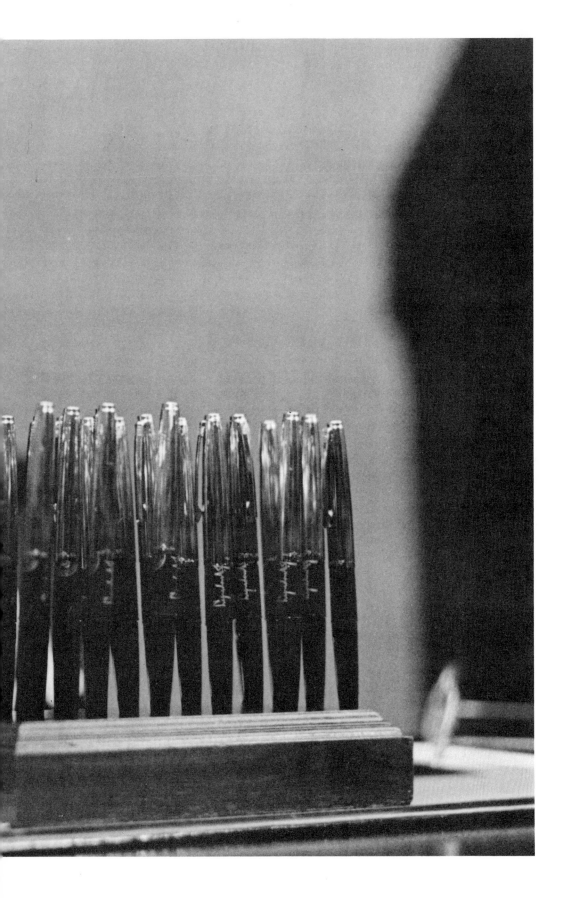

Lyndon himself, in his usual style, half humble, half extremely boastful, summed up the achievements best. In a long off-the-record conversation aboard his jet, Air Force One, he began by praising the "accomplishments of the last [89th] session" of Congress.

"I don't know how well they would have done on a vaudeville stage, because they are not on it," he said, "and they are not the stars on a gridiron, but I want to emphasize that in my thirty-five years in Washington I've never known men who are a better, super team in reasoning together. They work well with each other, with all members of the Cabinet, and I need not tell you that they work well with each other. I think it is important that if you want to evaluate and review that you keep that in perspective. These are not rookies who came up this year. McCormack came up in '28; only one man has been longer in the Senate, Hayden, and I'm not as old as he is. Russell and Byrd came up two years later. Of the 435 members [of Congress], 430 came after I was there.

"I remember so pleasantly that we met in the room with the Speaker. He never took a drink and I always took a drink. The Speaker and I [referring here to McCormack] nodded and winked trying to talk Rayburn into everything from the school bill to the minimum wage. McCormack and I saw everything much alike. I don't want to sound braggadocio, because I'm not entitled to the credit, but I doubt if any President has been served so well by his staff. No one has tried to be individual stars. It's been a coordinated operation, with liaison from the departments. Generally speaking, it's been an excellent job.

". . . Some of you may remember what your colleagues said at the beginning of the 89th Congress. They thought we had a great record, that we'd cleaned up Kennedy's program and therefore we'd be content to clean up the agenda of unfinished business and wait till '66 before making the big move. We passed eighty-six bills, seventeen of them for appropriations and the rest, everything from immigration to poverty, schools, and medical aid. I said to the leadership that it outdid the 59th Congress of Teddy Roosevelt, the 63d of Wilson, the 73d of FDR.

"Just as the legislation that those men passed in those periods is just now being fully realized, so will the harvest of the 89th be reaped a generation from now. A President and a Congress and a cabinet have to plow a long furrow for the next season's crops. That is what we did this year. Congress took many steps towards many long-range problems not yet faced up to before—rent supplements, teachers, beautification, doctors, every conceivable type of education, conservation, immigration, nurses, hospitals, cancer, heart, strokes, all kinds of research, twenty-four bills on education alone. On civil rights we have accomplished more in ten months than in all history put together. The same for conservation. We have many new concepts in agriculture, crime, and rapid rails, turning trains into planes, moving fast all over the country. I spent until midnight last night with the ICC members on transportation. Transportation will be a big problem next year. We are going to reorganize basic things.

"I ought to be very candid. We don't know the answers to a good many of these riddles. We don't know how to unpollute the water and desalt it, but we are trying to find out. We have got programs started and we are revving them up. We don't know if rent supplements are the answer. We don't have a complete program on how to clean the air and water. We are going to try and find out. The main point is that we are not standing still. We are moving forward. We can't wait until the final solutions are ready."

Then, after saying all that and much more, Lyndon had to outreach himself. He could not let the record stand as it was with his magnificent achievements in domestic affairs. He had to top it; he had to demonstrate his mastery not just of domestic, but foreign affairs.

Where he had indeed done best, he told the reporters, was in foreign affairs. There lay his finest achievements as America's President. He went so far as to speak contemptuously of Charles de Gaulle, that towering figure, saying "if he wants to jack off, he can."

Reading his words in our notes years later, we still get that strong sense of Lyndon's ego taking hold, of his desire to show the press—again—that their President was an international sophisticate skilled in the art and intricacies of diplomacy.

"You fellows had the idea we had done wonderful on the domestic front," he said to the reporters on his plane, in that session at the end of 1965, "but that the same thing is not true on the foreign front, because one little boy told you the day I took office that I was a little country boy, never been out of Johnson City, but that I understood domestic things. I think we have a good record in foreign affairs—*better* than domestic."

Then he ticked off some high spots: trouble, with Castro in the wings, in Brazil; trouble of the same kind in the Dominican Republic; trouble in the Congo; trouble with the Chinese fomenting revolutions in Africa. "But can you tell me one place where they succeeded?" All these were better since he had been President—and so were American relations with Great Britain and with France better under the Johnson era.

"Your country's not gone to hell," he said, somewhat belligerently. "Your foreign policy has not gone to hell."

Then Lyndon Johnson talked about Vietnam. There, too, the situation was "better."

"We are winning, we are not losing," said the President of the United States.

Vietnam.

The very name has come to be an epithet in the minds of millions of Americans. For Lyndon Johnson in the last years of his presidency it became an obsession. Vietnam divided his country. Vietnam drove him from office. Vietnam shattered his party. Vietnam besmirched his reputation and may have destroyed forever the monument of social and economic progress he hoped to leave for himself under the rubric of the Great Society.

There is enormous irony in all this. In later life Lyndon was to say that he had been haunted since childhood by the fear of "losing control," of being paralyzed and unable to react to great danger. That fear—although he never acknowledged it—was realized in his paralysis over Vietnam. Immobilized by the threat of World War III, he was prevented from inflicting a mortal wound on North Vietnam. Immobilized by the threat of Communist aggression elsewhere in Southeast Asia and in the world, he was prevented from withdrawing. He chose what he always believed was a moderate and restrained middle course, a compromise between radical options. That had been his method in the Senate and the basis of his legislative genius. But compromise in Vietnam proved fatal for him. Events took control.

Only once did he seem to recognize clearly what lay ahead if he "stayed on course" in Vietnam. It was in late 1964 at one of those stream-of-consciousness sessions with reporters where he could talk off the record and try to rationalize himself and his policies. No one, he said, "could mash a button" and end the war. But if we got out of Vietnam, disastrous results would follow. And so, he said, "I feel like a man floating on a piece of paper in the sea. If I got off that piece of paper, I would just be getting on another one." Either way, it was the sea and not the paper that would determine where he would land.

He had inherited from all the experience and history of his people and his own life a vision of America that was at once patriotic in the best and noble sense but also, at times, chauvinistic. He had said, for example, at the time of the Dominican intervention: "I have seen the glory of art in architecture," recalling a declamation he had given as a boy in Texas. "I have seen the sun rise on Mont Blanc. But the most beautiful vision that these eyes ever beheld was the flag of my country in a foreign land." He had also inherited, as he would constantly remind the country and his visitors, a great body of conventional wisdom about the war in Vietnam. It was the wisdom of the "best minds"—the Kennedy Cabinet, the academic community, the political community—that if South Vietnam were to fall all of Southeast Asia would fall and Communist aggression would be encouraged all around the world. That was also the wisdom of many of the great newspapers and magazines—the New York Times, the Washington Post, the Luce publications. They all endorsed the "domino theory" and urged Johnson, as they had urged Kennedy, to stand fast in Vietnam. There was no one to challenge this wisdom except the radical "pull-out boys" such as Wayne Morse (and no one listened to him) or the radical "big-bomb boys" such as General Le May (and no one listened to him). Who was Lyndon Johnson, "your cornpone President from the Deep South," to challenge Robert McNamara and McGeorge Bundy and the New York Times? The men he brought into the White House with him—the Valentis and McPhersons and Busbys and Watsons—did not challenge this received wisdom. It was not challenged by the Congress that approved the Gulf of Tonkin Resolution in 1964 and his every request for money and troops to pursue the war.

Nor for a long time was there any popular challenge to what he was doing. After the Tonkin Gulf incidents and the retaliatory bombing of North Vietnam, public approval of Johnson's Vietnam policies shot up to 71 per cent. When the bombings were resumed early in 1965, two-thirds of the people in the Gallup poll approved this intervention and a majority of those were willing for the country to pursue its efforts even at the risk of nuclear war. The commitment of Marines to the ground war in March and the large-scale commitment of infantry in the summer did not change these results. Support for the war policies remained high, as did Johnson's personal popularity. And the support was based primarily on the belief that the President knew better than anyone what should be done.

To Johnson, all this was "consensus." He had the "best minds" on his side, he had the national media, he had the Congress, and he had the people. It was true that antiwar teach-ins had been staged all across the country in the spring of 1965, that a few columnists urged more caution, that during the White House Festival of the Arts that summer John Hersey, Dwight MacDonald, Robert Lowell, Jules Feiffer, and a handful of others tried to embarrass him with antiwar statements.

119

But this was the bleating of stray lambs, Johnson thought, and he responded to it privately with irritation and patriotism. In a conversation with the *Post*'s Chalmers Roberts in March, 1965 (also quoted in *First Rough Draft*), he referred to his critics and then called for an aide to bring him three letters he had answered the night before:

They were from mothers of soldiers now in Vietnam—one from Virginia, one from Montana, and one from New York State. In each case the soldier had written home that things were going better than the stories said, that the U.S. should stick it out and could win, that the U.S. had better draw the line here or it wouldn't stick anywhere. After reading one emotional letter, together with the mother's words to Johnson on how she had been for negotiation and getting out but now had changed her mind, Johnson said:
"Now doesn't that make you [critics] feel like a shit-ass?"
. . . He is wrapped in the flag and means to back up the boys over there and not run out on them. An understanding of this emotion, I think, is fundamental to an understanding of his attitude toward Vietnam.

That emotion pervaded his thinking until he left the White House. And it was not shallow. When he made the decision in the summer of 1965 to fight on the ground in Vietnam, he spoke to the American people about the agony of taking that course:
"I do not find it easy to send the flower of our youth, our finest young men, into battle. I have spoken to you today of the divisions and the forces and battalions and the units, but I know them all, every one. I have seen them in a thousand streets, of a hundred towns, in every state of this union—working and laughing and building and filled with hope and life. I think I know, too, how their mothers weep and how their families sorrow."
Their deaths haunted him and hurt him because he *did* know them. Hugh Sidey of *Life* magazine wrote in March, 1968,

Lyndon Johnson comes from those people who mostly furnish the Pfcs and the Cpls who stand out there on the fringes of the Khe Sanh perimeter with a black M-16 and wait to be killed in the act of blunting the enemy's assaults . . . To Johnson each man is a Schultz or a Morsund or a Winters or a Croft out of Blanco County.

Sidey had flown with the President that day down to Fort Bragg, N.C. Airborne troops were loading up on transport planes, bound for Vietnam. Many of them had been there before. Many would not return. Johnson had come to say goodbye. He stood at the door of that plane, Sidey wrote,

and shook hands, murmuring, "Good luck" or "God bless you" as each got on. They were honored but their thoughts were beyond even the President of the United States. They were airborne troops. Major General Richard Seitz, commander of the 82nd Airborne Division, standing beside the President, kept shouting, "Airborne" or "All the way soldier" and it would stiffen their spines a bit because there was a huge pride going with the 82nd.

"O.K.," roared General Seitz, when the last man had gone in, "crank her up." Johnson put up a hand and held him up. He stepped inside and walked up the dim aisle in the fuselage. The men sat in silence with their weapons sticking up between their knees. If ever this war reached the heart of Lyndon Johnson, it did just then. "There are half a million men out there and they want you there. I know you will do well . . . I pray each of you comes back."

When he finished, they shouted, "All the way, sir," that airborne chant that is almost Boy Scoutish except when suddenly you need it and that was the time. The President lowered his eyes and walked up to the cabin and told the pilot, "Take care of those boys." That was another of those awful truths. They were so young. Then he hurried out of the plane and stuck his chin up and strode to his limousine. Before his car was off the airfield, the jet was whining and another was coming up to take its place on the ramp.

Death came to 1,369 of those boys in 1965; 5,008 in 1966; 9,378 in 1967; 14,592 in 1968. In total, 30,347 Schultzes, Morsunds, Winterses, and Crofts died under his command in Vietnam in those four years. Little wonder that he would rage at the critics and defend those boys who "shoulder their packs and face, not hostile placards and debating points, but the bullets and the mortar shells of marching aggressive armies." Little wonder that he would go out to Chicago in May, 1966, to declare: "The marines, the army, the airmen and the sailors who man the carriers off the coast of Vietnam tonight—they know no parties. They wear no Republican jackets or Democratic caps. . . . I do not believe that those men who are out there fighting for us tonight think that we should enjoy the luxury of fighting each other back home. . . . The road ahead is going to be difficult. There will be some 'Nervous Nellies' and some who will be frustrated and bothered and break ranks under the strain, and some will turn on their leaders, and on their country, and on our own fighting men . . . But . . . the wise American people will ultimately prevail. They will stand united until every boy is brought home safely, until the gallant people of South Vietnam have their own choice of their own government."

That, of course, was a delusion. His consensus already was breaking up. There was growing worry and dissatisfaction in Congress. The Schlesingers, Goodwins, and Galbraiths had begun to defect and speak out against the war. The newspapers and the television networks were painting a grim picture of death on a treadmill in jungles and rice paddies. Students were taking to the streets, rioting on campuses. The draft-card burnings had begun. Two young men had immolated themselves in protest to the war. The congressional elections that fall produced severe defeats for the Democrats. Pickets were outside the White House and the President began hearing that ugly, hurtful chant: "Hey, hey, LBJ! How many kids did you kill today?"

Now they were dying by the hundreds in Vietnam. The draft calls were rising. Thousands of troops were still pouring in. And still the President "stayed on course." He sat in the White House reading and passing on all those hopeful and optimistic reports from the Westmorelands, McNamaras, Rostows, and Rusks:

"We have stopped losing the war." (McNamara, 1965)

"I expect . . . the war to achieve very sensational results in 1967." (Lodge, 1967)

"We have reached an important point when the end begins to come into view . . . the enemy's hopes are bankrupt." (Westmoreland, 1967)

It was being said then and would be said later that Johnson "lied" to the American people, that he withheld the "real" facts, that he knew the war was going badly and that he kept going nevertheless for reasons never explained. But there is no evidence in support of judgments like that. He talked the same way privately. Whenever reporters got to see him on a personal basis in those days he would invariably reassure them that things were going well. He would read from the secret reports he was getting. And only occasionally would he ever hear dissent inside the White House.

One of those occasions was in August, 1967. He invited some reporters to the yellow Oval Room in the White House living quarters. The talk went on for more than two hours. He explained the care he was taking to avoid provocations to China, he discussed the targets in North Vietnam he had decided to hit, he referred to relations with Russia ("Vietnam is almost as much a burden to the Russians as to us"), then he talked about the Saigon government, headed by Thieu and Ky. It was the most recent of a series of regimes in South Vietnam and Johnson observed:

"If you've had five maids and they are all dreadful and feed your child carbolic acid you are mighty eager to hold on to one who is reliable even if she has a few faults. So it is with Thieu and Ky . . . On instructions of ours we assassinated Diem and then, by God, I walked into it. It was too late and we went through one government after another. The press people are very unhappy with the government. But no one I have sent out there can find anyone better than Thieu and Ky. Ky is a damn fool in some ways but I don't know anyone better out there. I have a somewhat higher opinion of Thieu. He's not so flamboyant. . . .

"I don't know how in hell to get out. Hanoi is not in the slightest interested in any discussion . . . I'll tell you just between ourselves that the most difficult thing we face—and it's not the bombing problem or the Mansfield criticism or anything like that—is to survive a coup and get an honest election. If that [coup] happens, I think I'll resign and let Hubert have it."

At one point he began reading from a progress report from his generals in Vietnam—statistics of roads cleared, population under government control, enemy losses, improvements in the army of South Vietnam. It went on and on. Suddenly, Lady Bird Johnson, who had been listening silently, blurted out, with evident bitterness, "That's not what I've been reading in the papers."

That isn't what the American people had been reading either, and the difference showed up in the polls. By that time—two years after the commitment of ground troops to Southeast Asia—Johnson's popularity in the country had plummeted unbelievably—from 70 per cent approval of his policies and performance in 1965 to 39 per cent in August, 1967. He was as unloved as poor Harry Truman had been at the end of his term when he was saddled with "Communism, Korea, and Corruption."

The revolt of the intellectuals by now was more than an annoyance. The campuses were in turmoil over the war. The liberal journals, day after day, poured out their criticisms and denunciations of the man in the White House. The ultimate insult was the MacBeth parody *MacBird*, written by Barbara Garson, a graduate of the University of California at Berkeley, one of the great centers of anti-Johnson, antiwar dissent. MacBird was Lyndon and he was depicted thus:

Messenger: *Beatniks burning draft*
          cards.
MacBird: *Jail 'em.*
Messenger: *Negroes starting sit-ins.*
MacBird: *Gas 'em.*
Messenger: *Latin rebels rising.*
MacBird: *Shoot 'em.*
Messenger: *Asian peasants arming.*
MacBird: *Bomb 'em.*
Messenger: *Congressmen complaining.*
MacBird: *Fuck 'em.*
          Flush out this filthy
          scum; destroy dissent.
          It's treason to defy your
          President.
          You heard me! Get on,
          get your ass in gear.
          Get rid of all this protest
          stuff, y'hear?

Dwight MacDonald reviewed *MacBird* for the *New York Review of Books*. He called it "the funniest, toughest-minded, and most ingenious satire I've read in years . . . " His attitude revealed, in exaggerated form, the gulf that had developed between Johnson and the writers, artists, and scholars who symbolized the American intellectual establishment. Lyndon felt as strongly about them, and occasionally there would be a counterattack. In the fall of 1966, John Roche, who had succeeded Eric Goldman as the White House "intellectual-in-residence," spoke out in an interview. The President's intellectual critics, he said, "are only a small body of self-appointed people who live in affluent alienation on Cape Cod and fire off salvos against the vulgarity of the masses . . . The main problem is that an awful lot of these guys prefer style to performance." He went on to identify these critics:

Mainly the New York arts-craftsy set. They're in the *Partisan Review* and the *New York Review of Books* and publications like that. The West Side Jack-albins, I call them. They intend to launch a revolution from Riverside Drive. . . . [They] are mainly high class illiterates. A story by Irving Howe,

124

for example, should be edited with flea powder.

The truth was that the great gulf between Johnson and these writers and scholars and publishers was merely a symptom of the great gulf that had arisen in the country over the war. It was a divided country, as the President finally recognized, and the power of the opposition was such that it produced serious challenges to his leadership from Eugene McCarthy and Robert Kennedy in the primaries of 1968.

But by that time it was all over for him. The war had been, as he had sensed in his heart and mind before he embarked on it, a great and unmanageable sea that would sweep him along to triumph or tragedy. It swept him to tragedy. He had been helpless against the tide. He had lost control of events.

During all his years in the White House Lyndon kept dropping private hints that he would not run again. No one believed him, of course. But the evidence was there.

There had been that charade, before the Atlantic City convention, when he said he had been talked out of not seeking the nomination by Lady Bird. There had been the time, in late 1964, when he told Carroll Kilpatrick: "Maybe the country needs a new man as President, one with fewer scars than I have." There had been the days, in '65, when Eric Goldman told us: "The President keeps telling his staff he won't run again, but I don't think anyone should believe this." There had been that rest period in mid-'66 when he invited Henry Luce of the Time Inc. publishing empire down to the ranch. "I don't know if I can hold the country together with my background," he told Luce.

In all these years he had expressed private doubts about his ability to do the job and about his own background. Once, when talking about his counterpart in South Vietnam, he said wearily: "Like me, maybe he comes from the wrong region, maybe he doesn't have needed abilities, but he's trying to pull the country together."

Looking back now on his comments over that period, it is surprising to find how many times he voiced frustration with the presidency. He couldn't move freely; he couldn't really meet the people; he was limited socially; he wished, wistfully, he could go up to a little room in the Capitol and plan strategy with the leaders as he had in the old days; he yearned for the pleasures and rewards of the Senate leadership; and he talked about wanting to go back to Texas after so many years, to teach young people.

There were other signs of strain as the Johnson years became associated with so much turmoil both at home and abroad. He became increasingly defensive and hypersensitive to criticism. He displayed more and more secretiveness and truculence. He slept less. He began to see conspiracies mounted against him. Inevitably, these strains affected his relations with the press, his staff, his old congressional colleagues, and, ultimately, the American people.

The press was a special problem. He had begun his presidency telling the reporters who covered him daily in the White House that he wanted to make "big men" out of them. But by the time his policies had come under attack and the war was beginning to consume him he reacted sharply, and often with cruel personal statements. There was the time, for instance, when one of his aides told him that Merriman Smith of the UPI—one of those he was going to make "big"—was inquiring whether the President would be returning Sunday or Monday from Camp David. Around 9 o'clock at night the aide's home phone rang. It was Lyndon.

"I hear you are trying to find out when I am returning to Washington."

"Yes, sir. The reporters up there called me and just wanted to know whether they should be prepared to stay overnight."

"That's none of their Goddamn business," the President replied.

"Smitty saw what he thought were helicopters arriving, and so he asked me to find out," the aide said.

Merriman Smith had once had a drinking problem, and had conquered it, and Lyndon knew that. "Tell Smitty it wasn't helicopters he saw, but snakes," Lyndon said.

Then there was the day at the ranch during a Christmas holiday, when Lyndon asked another aide if any additional reporters had arrived, and the aide said, referring to the columnist Robert Novak, "Bob Novak is here, I am told, but I haven't seen him." That was when Lyndon said, "See him? You don't have to see him. You can smell him."

Novak had become one of his chief hates, and for a typically Johnsonian reason. He was continually remarking that when Novak married a Johnson secretary, he, Lyndon, gave a huge wedding reception for them. Yet Novak now wrote nasty things about him. Novak, obviously, was ungrateful. He should have been writing *nice* things.

In the more peaceful period of his presidency, when everything was going well and he was being hailed as another Roosevelt, Lyndon delighted in showing his visitors all the Johnson headlines in the *Post, Times, Herald-Tribune, Evening Star, Baltimore Sun,* and *Philadelphia Inquirer* that he kept near his desk on a table in the Oval Office. He also liked to tell how he had seen Johnson clips on the Huntley-Brinkley or Walter Cronkite television news shows.

Later, in a more divisive time, he would read aloud typed excerpts of press reports to show how superficial and inaccurate they were, or mimic TV commentators with elaborate sarcasm.

Part of the problem was that Lyndon, unlike other presidents, was an inveterate reader of the press and an insatiable watcher of TV. He read it all and he saw it all, and as time went on the more he read and the more he saw the less he liked. There was a masochistic quality in his behavior. He knew that he was being called, as he said once, a "Hitler and a murderer," but he kept on seeing and reading what was being reported about him. He devoured it all and, like a wounded elk, bellowed and bled but kept going back for more. What he was seeing, as his problems mounted, were scenes of shouting demonstrators across the country holding up their placards and shouting their obscenities at *him,* of bloody battles in Vietnam and inflated "body counts" and critics assailing *his* war, of respected congressional leaders attacking *his* integrity.

Lyndon had an obsession about the media. He loved it, he hated it, he could not ignore it. In his White House bedroom, he kept three TV sets lined up on a rack, one for each network with the network numbers under each set. He would carry a remote control switch in his hand that enabled him to turn on all three pictures at once or switch at will from one network to another. Every night he would listen to the 11 o'clock news on all three networks as he got his evening rubdown on a table set up in his bedroom.

His relations with his staff became increasingly difficult and complex. Lyndon never was an easy man to work for. He drove people mercilessly, and he was capable of petty slights and cruelties. Early in his Administration he walked into the office of Malcolm Kilduff, a Kennedy holdover, looked at Kilduff's desk, which was neat and empty, and said: "Kilduff, I hope your mind is not as empty as your desk." A few days later, he again walked into Kilduff's office. This time he saw several papers on the desk. "Kilduff, clean up your desk," he snapped, and walked out.

One summer day, when trying to get more of his private polls to prove to a reporter how popular he was, he ordered Jack Valenti to have Walter Jenkins bring in the material. Jenkins had gone to the beach, he was told. "Jenkins' wife has gone off to the beach," Lyndon told the reporter cuttingly, "and Walter had to go running after her." He then ordered Valenti to get James Rowe on the phone. When Valenti was unable to reach Rowe, Johnson was furious. "Tell him to always leave his phone number with the White House operator," LBJ commanded.

Once, he gave Joseph Laitin, an assistant White House press secretary, a handsome transistor radio. Some days later Laitin's home phone rang at 7:30 in the morning. Lyndon was upset. He wanted to know if Laitin had heard what CBS had said about him on the 7 A.M. news. Laitin said he had missed the broadcast.

"What were you doing?" Lyndon asked.

"I was busy with something else," Laitin replied. "I plan to listen to the 8 o'clock news."

"Don't you think you ought to listen to the 7 o'clock?"

"Yes, sir."

"Didn't I give you a radio a couple of weeks ago?"

"Yes, sir. It is a very good one, I appreciate it."

"Well, if you aren't going to use it, give it back to me," Lyndon said, and hung up.

In the way of gossipy Washington, a number of these incidents slipped into print. Others made the rounds of Georgetown and Cleveland Park parties and were passed by word of mouth in the most influential circles. When Lyndon's selfless assistant, Jack Valenti, made an effusive speech about the President all Washington exploded in laughter. Valenti described Lyndon as a sensitive and cultivated man, a great visionary "who hones in on the nerve-edges of the issue," a President who welcomes dissent. "I sleep each night a little better, a little more confidently, because Lyndon Johnson is my President," he said.

A few days later Washington was laughing again at Lyndon's expense when Herblock drew a cartoon in the *Washington Post* of three cringing White House staffers, bare to the waist, their backs deeply slashed, while the President walked away, bullwhip in hand. "Happy Days on the Old Plantation," Herblock entitled his cartoon.

As his problems became more serious, and as a number of key White House assistants left, Lyndon turned on them cuttingly. George Reedy, whom he once said was the man closest to him, left as press secretary and was disparaged. Bill Moyers, his "son," took the job, and then he went too, and he too was described in harsh terms. "Moyers is not a foreign policy expert. I never had one hour's discussion of foreign policy with Moyers," he told us in May of 1967. "I have had ten times that amount with George Christian." (Christian was his latest press secretary.) Moyers could go out to Hickory Hill and dance the Watusi and fall in the pool with the Kennedys. In Lyndon's view, Moyers was flirting with the Kennedys. That was unforgivable.

When McGeorge Bundy left and his major functions were assumed by Walt Rostow, Lyndon responded with more of the same. "Bundy was a little more flippant and humorous and social and held more backgrounders," he said. "I wouldn't give him a rating over Rostow at all. I asked Kennedy if I could see Bundy after the Bay of Pigs and he said Bundy was too upset for several days to see anyone. Rostow keeps his head. It's a slander to call him a hawk. He is an eagle. Where is the presidential seal? He carries an olive branch and an arrow. I have never seen him cut anyone up or criticize a person. He gives both sides of everything."

When George Ball left, he was denounced, in yet another private session,

Happy Days On The Old Plantation

L.B.J. IS "A SENSITIVE MAN, A CULTIVATED MAN, A WARM-HEARTED MAN... I SLEEP EACH NIGHT A LITTLE BETTER, A LITTLE MORE CONFIDENTLY BECAUSE LYNDON JOHNSON IS MY PRESIDENT." — speech by Jack Valenti.

for "leaking" documents to a writer critical of Lyndon. When Richard Goodwin left—Goodwin, whom he had called "wonderful, that boy . . . " —Johnson rendered a passionate indictment: Dick Goodwin, whom he had helped when his wife was sick, Dick Goodwin, who had told Lyndon he was the greatest man he ever knew, Dick Goodwin, who "was never in on anything related to Vietnam. Now he is a Vietnam expert!"

Finally, Robert McNamara left. McNamara, once his most admired assistant, "that lard-hair man," in Lyndon's affectionate term, "the most competent man I ever knew . . . the most objective man I ever met." After he was gone, there were no more comments about the great McNamara. It was Dean Rusk who was receiving the lavish LBJ encomiums: "the greatest Secretary of State in this century."

Lyndon's problem with the dissenters was similar: Before the climate became so venomous, he tended to take their criticism more philosophically. "People like to fuss at their President," he would say in his private meetings, "the way they fuss at the bus driver; he's either too early or too late. And the press likes to play up controversy." Or he would talk about other periods of national stress, of William Jennings Bryan resigning from Wilson's cabinet in opposition to World War I, of the Neutrality Act before World War II, of Senator Robert Taft criticizing Truman after Korea. "I lived through all that and I know it, though lots of the younger people don't. From what little history I know I don't think it's really different from Washington or Lincoln or the rest and what they had to face." But later he showed a darker side. Lyndon "sees Communists everywhere," one of his White House aides said. "Ambassador Dobrynin [of the Soviet Union] seems to have more votes in the Senate" than the President of the United States, the President complained. And strictly in confidence he let it be known that he sat up in his bed at night reading secret FBI reports about who went to what embassy party and talked with what senator or writer and what Communist emissaries were present. Once, while walking around the White House grounds, he alluded to J. Edgar Hoover's reporting to him regularly about "all these Vietnam rallies in the country," about who was planning them, and what were their motives. It sounded as though anyone opposed to his policies was suspect, and dossiers on them were being built up, as indeed it turned out there were.

As for his congressional critics, they were his own "little group of willful men." "They'd rather fight me than the enemy."

He began raging that he could not control the State Department and, in a bitter personal confrontation with Robert Kennedy, he said, in accusatory tones, it's your State Department, and your Defense Department, not mine. He was aware that he was losing control.

The strain showed. Lyndon aged visibly. Suddenly, his hair was grayer, the lines in his face were more deeply etched, and he often looked exhausted. Normally, he would get up about 6 every morning and work on papers in his bedroom, take a nap in midafternoon, then work again, sometimes until 1 or 2 in the morning. But as the war news became worse, he got in the habit of waking up about 3 o'clock every morning to call the White House situation room for Vietnam reports.

"Almost every morning at 3 o'clock," his brother, Sam Houston, wrote,

he would crawl out of bed, often without ever having gone to sleep, wearily slip on his robe and slippers, then go down to the situation room in the basement of the White House to get the latest reports coming from Saigon. Even the loss of one soldier (it was never that few) could bring on a mood of sadness and frustrated anger that would keep him awake the rest of the night.

Sitting down at breakfast with him and Lady Bird, I could always tell what kind of news had come in from Vietnam. There would be dark hollows under his eyes, his face appeared somewhat gray and drawn, his shoulders slumped forward, his voice was slightly raspy. Pretending not to know he had had another restless worried night, I would try to make light conversation about any silly thing that came to mind. It seldom did any good. His mood remained somber and uncommunicative.

His health was a source of constant speculation and concern. In 1965 he had a gall bladder operation, and the next year underwent double surgery for removal of a polyp and repair of a ventural hernia. Always in the background was the threat left by the massive heart attack he had had in 1955 when he was Majority Leader. He began having recurring dreams about losing control, about being stricken like Woodrow Wilson in the White House and, he later told a friend, about hearing his aides discussing how they would divide "my" power. He could count on none of them, it appeared. It was after these dreams, he said, that he would get up and prowl the halls of the darkened White House with a flashlight looking for the portrait of Wilson.

At a dinner party one night at Senator Mike Monroney's house he told of his anguished state of mind at a time when American air strikes in North Vietnam had set off another round of attacks on his policies, there were general fears of a still wider war developing, and the specter of Chinese intervention loomed large. His daughter Luci came in one night and looked at him. "You are worrying," he said she told him. "Your brow looks like it's been plowed." Lyndon told her of the Vietnam situation, and said: "What we need is some hard and deep praying."

"Let's go and see my little monks," Luci suggested. At this period, she had been studying to become a Catholic and often went to pray at St. Dominic's in Washington. Although it was after 1 o'clock in the morning, they got Lady Bird out of bed, summoned a White House limousine, and drove off in the night to pray with the monks.

Later, on a number of other occasions—including the day Lyndon announced he would not seek another term—Luci took her father and mother to St. Dominic's for a private prayer session.

The pressures and the problems kept mounting. Then it was 1968, and the blows came swiftly and cruelly, one after another—the first on the morning of January 23, when the USS *Pueblo* was seized by the North Koreans. Lyndon later was to say: "It formed the first link in a chain that added up to one of the most agonizing years any President has ever spent in the White House."

Those tumultuous events of 1968 are too well known to be retold here—

from the *Pueblo* to the massive Tet offensive to the New Hampshire primary and Eugene McCarthy to the Robert Kennedy candidacy (again, a Kennedy overshadowing Lyndon) to the terrible days of Vietnam reappraisal in March and finally to Lyndon's stunning announcement on March 31 that he would not seek the presidency again and had set in motion the de-escalation process in Vietnam.

He gave one glimpse of his inner turmoil during that time that is worth recording. Immediately after the New Hampshire primary, he called reporters into his private cabin on Air Force One while he was flying from Austin, Texas, to Minneapolis. He was asked if he thought public support for the war had increased or decreased since the Tet offensive.

"I don't know," he said. "There are a lot of people in this country working full time around the clock to lose this war for us in this country. There are a good many people who are powerful and influential who would like to see

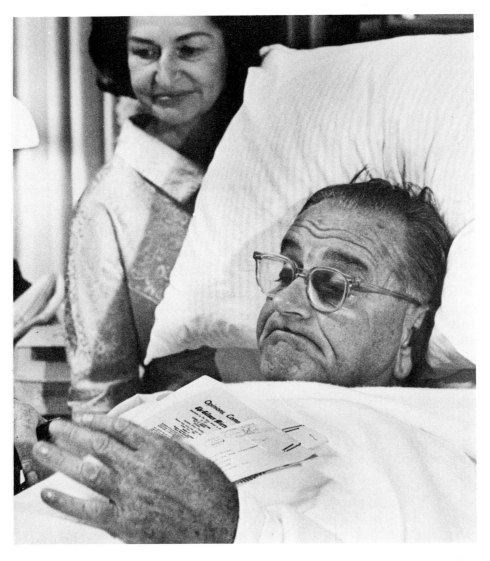

us pull out and quit. I believe they had this feeling all through but it is coming through now and they are becoming more vociferous. It must be significant that you see very few stories on how Ho broke the truce. I think that was a dastardly thing. If we had done it it would have run for days and days. He has broken every truce, everything every schoolboy should know. It is significant this was not stressed in the press. They have more hope of winning the war in Washington than they do in Vietnam. You stress corruption one week, Thieu the next. All these things are done to discredit us. Well-intentioned, patriotic people sometimes are involved, but sometimes people on the other side are trying to discredit us, people from Eastern Europe, for example."

Then he said:

"It doesn't make any difference who causes you to jump out the window after you jump."

Lyndon also spoke that day of Robert Kennedy. "Bobby was a real hawk about Vietnam a few years ago," he said. "Why don't the papers point this out?"

In his own mind, he must have believed he knew the answer before posing the question. It was another example of the "conspiracy" against him, another case of his being dealt with unfairly by the Kennedy crowd and their admirers in the media.

He was, of course, extremely thin-skinned about what he often called the "Georgetown liberal set" and sometimes for months nursed imagined slights from those he took to be its members—as Ben Bradlee, the editor of the *Washington Post*, learned on a later occasion.

Bradlee had seen Lyndon privately at night in the White House not long after Robert McNamara resigned. Lyndon was acutely aware that Washington was full of gossip that McNamara's departure was another defection to the Kennedy camp. He also knew that Bradlee, a New Englander and Harvard graduate, for years had been one of John Kennedy's closest friends and a Georgetown neighbor. Bradlee asked the President if it were true that General Earle (Buzz) Wheeler had replied "bull shit" when queried about a news report that the Joint Chiefs of Staff were going to quit unless McNamara was fired. Lyndon said no, and their conversation turned into one of those long, rambling sessions journalists often had with him. It had been pleasant, Bradlee thought.

But some time afterward, when Lyndon was on an Asian swing, he summoned the reporters aboard Air Force One to his cabin and, to their astonishment, in the plane high over Thailand, went into a long account of that meeting with Bradlee months before. He began by recalling how he told Bradlee to "come on over. I got nothing else to do this evening." Then he launched into one of his famous imitations. "Ben Bradlee sits there," he said, "with that Stacomb in his hair, wringing his hands and asking is it true that Buzz Wheeler said 'bull shit' when asked if the Joint Chiefs were going to quit." Lyndon paused for effect, then, leaning forward dramatically, proclaimed loudly: "What I want to know is how come when I say it it comes out Bull Shit and when Bradlee says it it comes out Ch-an-elllll Number F-a-h-v?"

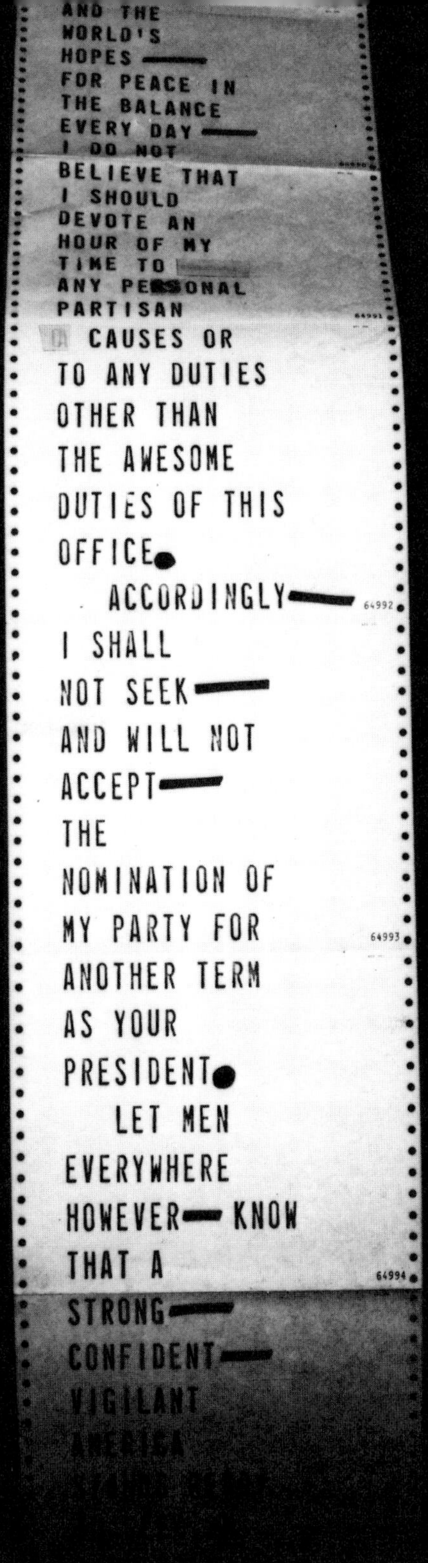

AND THE
WORLD'S
HOPES ——
FOR PEACE IN
THE BALANCE
EVERY DAY ——
I DO NOT
BELIEVE THAT
I SHOULD
DEVOTE AN
HOUR OF MY
TIME TO
ANY PERSONAL
PARTISAN

CAUSES OR
TO ANY DUTIES
OTHER THAN
THE AWESOME
DUTIES OF THIS
OFFICE.
    ACCORDINGLY ——
I SHALL
NOT SEEK ——
AND WILL NOT
ACCEPT ——
THE
NOMINATION OF
MY PARTY FOR
ANOTHER TERM
AS YOUR
PRESIDENT.
    LET MEN
EVERYWHERE
HOWEVER —— KNOW
THAT A
STRONG ——
CONFIDENT ——
VIGILANT
AMERICA

On April 1, the day after his dramatic announcement that he would not seek the presidency again, Lyndon was in an entirely different mood. He felt a great sense of relief after announcing his decision. He reminisced about old days on Capitol Hill. If he had his druthers maybe he'd still like to be the leader, but he had his family to think of in the years he had left to live. It would be fine to be a senator from Texas for life, but he couldn't be selfish. He spoke of the frustrations of the presidency. The load was unbearable. "It's getting to the point where a President can no longer be President." But he was content. He had had a full life, and a happy one. He had done everything he ever wanted to, he had enjoyed it, and he had served the public. It was wonderful to be flying off to Chicago and not be accused of cheap political moves. "No one can say I'm going there for political reasons, or that I'm trying to get Daley in a corner, or trying to line up delegates. I don't have to carry that sack of cement now. I can throw it off." Now he was looking forward to retirement. He might even learn to play bridge, and he would teach young people again, and camp out on the ranch and see the bluebonnets when they came up in the spring. He had had problems, sure, but as a Johnson City boy he had gone as far as you could go—and he had done a pretty good job for a Johnson City boy. He was about the luckiest guy who ever lived.

And now he could relax and enjoy himself in the last months of his presidency. The burden had been lifted.

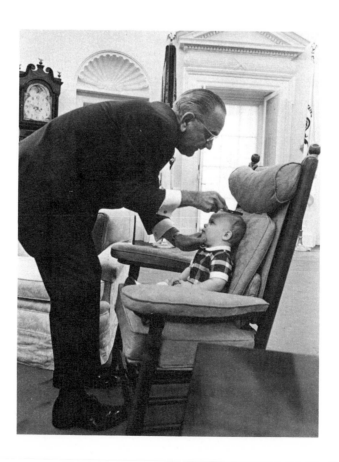

But it wasn't. Within three days, Martin Luther King had been assassinated. A wave of riots swept the country. The nation's capital itself was in flames, and soldiers were posted around the very walls of the White House to protect the President. The war kept getting worse, and it was still his war. By early May he looked dreadful, battered and stumbling over his words, driven to the point of physical collapse. His words reflected his appearance: he was gloomy, and the bitterness came through. "The only difference between the Kennedy assassination and mine is that I am alive and it has been more tortuous," he said, on another plane ride that spring. He also said: "The only people more bigoted than the Georgetown intellectual set are a few people in Mississippi."

Then came another bullet in the night and another Kennedy lay slain and another period of national mourning began with another cortege moving to the somber slopes of Arlington. "Oh, my God!" Lyndon said, when he was awakened in the White House to be told Robert Kennedy had been assassinated. "Not again. Don't tell me it's happened all over again."

The Chicago Democratic convention was not his convention. It was, again, a vast memorial to the Kennedys, and a vicious outpouring of hatred against Lyndon Johnson. "Fuck you, LBJ!" the demonstrators chanted in the street. "Pull out like your daddy should have."

Lyndon was not there, but somehow you knew he heard.

By Labor Day, as the presidential campaign began, Lyndon's popularity had fallen to its all-time low point. Only 35 per cent of the American people, Gallup reported, thought their President was doing an acceptable job.

In those last months of his presidency Lyndon Johnson hardly existed in the minds of his countrymen. He was already through, a figure consigned to a bitter past. His party's nominee, Hubert Humphrey, the man he had given a chance at presidential succession, studiedly ignored him. Democrats campaigning for office would not mention his name. The pollsters did not rate his popularity. They did not need to; his presidency notwithstanding, he was no longer a force on the American scene.

Lyndon intruded into the American consciousness only once in those final days. On October 31, just a few days before the election, he announced he was calling a complete halt to all American air, naval, and artillery bombardment of North Vietnam in order to give a better chance for the peace negotiations in Paris. He was immediately denounced for playing partisan politics.

He had one final private moment with a *Washington Post* reporter before he left office. At the end of November, during a White House social reception, he invited several women reporters present to come upstairs for a drink. One of them was Judith Martin of the *Post*. The President was gracious, and in one of his loquacious moods. It was a reminiscent Lyndon who appeared that night. As usual, what he said was completely off the record. He spoke first of the ordeal of the vice-presidency.

"My father used to say to me, 'Son, you never know what it is to be in someone else's position until you're in it.' No one knows what it is to be President until he is, and no one knows what it is to be Vice President, thank God, until he is. Everyone wants to talk to the President, get his quotes, but you sit there like a bump on a log, trying not to get in the way. You have no authority, no power, no decisions to make, but you have to abide by the decisions another man makes. If you're independent, you're disloyal, and if not, you're a stooge or a puppet. If you're a governor of a state [referring to Spiro T. Agnew of Maryland], you're Mr. It, with Number One on your license plates. But he's going to find it hard to be Vice President.

"President Kennedy worked so hard to give me dignity, but in the background everybody was quoting Bobby and Nixon saying I'd be thrown off the ticket. The last thing President Kennedy said to me, in front of my sister and her husband—he was putting on his shirt and then he got on that plane—the last thing he told me was, 'We're going to carry two states, if we don't do anything else.' And they were Massachusetts and Texas."

He mentioned how everyone had always assumed he craved power. That wasn't true; it was a myth. When he became President, in that awful period of tragedy, he remembered his wife, Bird, telling him, "We'll do the best we can, we'll do all we can in four years, but let's don't get involved and die in the office." "We had horrible memories of my heart attack in 1955 and heart attacks of others," he said. "My blood pressure was down to zero, and I came back . . . I saw what happened to Senator Kerr, and others. I saw Woodrow Wilson here as an invalid. I'm in excellent health now. I'm going to sign 200 letters tonight, and I worked until 2 o'clock this morning."

He was satisfied. "Haven't we achieved everything a human being can do? Do we need an airplane? We have one. The White House? We have a house we enjoy better than this one. When history looks back on this period, it'll see unrest and violence. I used the United States Army a great many times . . . Selma, Resurrection City. But we haven't killed anybody."

Here he became highly agitated, and, waving his hand in the ladies' faces, said: "Whatever power I've had, I've used it. I've used it for good. I've tried to use it for human beings." Moments later, he became quite emotional again while talking about the way he would conduct himself as President right up till the end. "I'm going to be in charge right up till the last minute," he said, almost shouting the words.

Then he calmed down as he thought again about the retirement days to come. "I'm just going to love it, don't worry. I'm going to have an exciting life, a wonderful time." He might have "five to ten years of activity," and he wanted to spend it partly by teaching and helping provide scholarships for those who could not afford an education.

"I'm going to have an office at San Marcos," he said, referring to the small college where he had studied years before. "They've been awfully kind to me. They let me sweep their main building for $30 a year for two years. Maybe I'll find some janitor there and give him a chance."

January 20, 1969, the Capitol: Gray, somber, a chill bite in the air, the wind whipping the flags over the Capitol dome and the platform set up on the steps of the east front. No sign of the sunshine that had graced the three previous inaugurals, but the cast was familiar. Many of them had been there exactly eight years before: Richard Nixon, then the outgoing Vice President, his political career presumably finished; Lyndon Johnson, then the incoming Vice President, just about to step onto history's stage; Senator Hubert Humphrey, who was to become Vice President and defeated presidential candidate in his own right, Chief Justice Earl Warren, his white hair again ruffled by the wind, about to administer the oath in the ceremonial black robes of his office.

The Marine Band, resplendent in bright red uniforms, struck up "Hail to the Chief" for Lyndon's last time as President. He took his place on the platform. They played "The Yellow Rose of Texas." Then there was a salute to the new President, then a pause, and the assembled leaders of the American Government took their seats. It was colder now, and Richard Nixon handed Lyndon a blanket to ward off the chill. As he turned, he quietly asked Lyndon how he felt. With that half smile so characteristic of him always, Lyndon replied:

"This is the happiest day of my life."

The Last Years

Lyndon was a child of the small-town, American middle class that has been celebrated or sneered at in countless novels and sociological studies: Babbitt's class. He might have prospered and found peace as a merchant or banker and part-time politician in Johnson City or Austin, hunting and fishing on the weekends, poker sessions with old friends, a small ranch to occupy the idle time, a sense of place and identity.

He became, instead, the President of the United States, the "leader of the free world," the Commander-in-Chief of vast armies and fleets, the focus of mass hopes and mass fears. Few men who have led such a kingly existence and exercised such power find it easy to go home again.

Lyndon's case was particularly complicated.

No matter how many problems they have encountered in office, no matter how unpopular they may have been as their terms ended, Presidents traditionally have been accorded special respect in their retirement, and it has often been accorded by Americans who reviled them when they were in office. Harry Truman, the object of so much scorn in his last presidential years, quickly saw the public view of him change as he became a private citizen. When Truman left Washington to return home to Independence, a crowd of 9,000 people jammed Union Station to bid him a fond farewell. Another 10,000 were on hand to greet him in Missouri, and 5,000 more surrounded his house to cheer him. "If this is what you get for all those years of hard work I guess it was worth it," his wife, Bess, told him. Herbert Hoover, discounted, distrusted, indeed hated, as he left office in the midst of the Depression, also lived to enjoy a surprisingly kind public judgment. He became an elder statesman. Dwight Eisenhower, admired and popular in the Presidency, was venerated in his retirement years. Even those who had belittled him began to express respect and appreciation for his presidency. In 1972 the Democratic presidential nominee, George McGovern, hailed Eisenhower as his model. Some of our former presidents spent their last years in renewed political activity. For seventeen years John Quincy Adams served with distinction as a member of Congress. Theodore Roosevelt formed a new political party, ran again for President, and continued an active political life until his death in 1919.

Lyndon was not so fortunate.

As he returned to private life he was repudiated and reviled as perhaps no leader in our history. Lyndon, the conciliator, the man of consensus, the compleat politician, was leaving behind him an America more deeply divided than at any point since the Civil War. At home, there were still riots and fears of a revolution in the streets. Abroad, America was still deeply embroiled in its most unpopular war. And Lyndon, who craved affection and attention, left Washington knowing he had been unable to travel freely in his country without fear of insult—or worse. He would continue to be scorned, would continue to hear the sounds of protest and criticism in the years he had left to live.

Although he would speak, in his first year back on the ranch, of how happy he was and how much he was enjoying life, he never would find peace. He would also say, both privately and publicly, that he had never really wanted power, never really wanted to be President, never really thought he possessed the necessary qualities for the job. It was always clear to him, he reflected in those days, that he had "certain disadvantages" that affected his ability to lead the nation: his upbringing, his limited educational background, his place of birth, his accent and what he had described as "the prejudices that exist." He had, he said, "a general inability to stimulate, inspire, and unite all the people of the country, which I think is an essential function of the presidency."

He added:

"Now I never believed that I was the man to do that particular job."

And:

"I always felt that every job I ever had was really too big for me."

As he should have expected, those remarks brought further abuse. To the end, he was not believed.

One story that he told repeatedly, had told earlier, and developed at length in his memoirs, brought special disbelief. Apparently as a way of proving that he never relished presidential power, he said over and over again that he had decided in 1964 not to accept his party's nomination. It wasn't true, as everyone had believed, that he wanted to win in his own name and own right. No, he never desired that. He wanted out. It was Bird who changed his mind, Bird who posed the alternatives in decisively specific terms. As he quoted her in his book:

"You will have various ranch lands, small banking interests, and presumably the TV to use up your talents and your hours. They are chicken-feed compared to what you are used to. That may be relaxing for a while. I think it is

144

not enough for you at 56. And I dread seeing you semi-idle, frustrated, looking back at what you left. I dread seeing you look at Mr. X running the country and thinking you could have done it better. You may look around for a scape-goat. I do not want to be it. You may drink too much—for lack of a higher calling."

He faced the same prospect on January 20, 1969, as his presidency ended. On that day, he later recalled, he felt a sense of liberation and great relief. In an interview months later with Walter Cronkite, he told of an inaugural day conversation with the new President:

President Nixon said to me, "How did you feel when you weren't President any more?" And I said, "I don't know whether you'll understand this now or not, but you certainly will later. I sat there on that platform and waited for you to stand up and raise your right hand and take the oath of office, and I think the most pleasant words that . . . ever came to my ears were 'So help me God' that you repeated after that oath." Because at that time I no longer had the fear that I was the man who could make the mistake of involving the world in war, that I was no longer the man that would have to carry the terrifying responsibility of protecting the lives of this country and maybe the entire world, unleashing the horrors of some of our great power if I felt that was required.

He had other fears, however. He was only sixty years old. His health was good, and those enormous energies and appetites still churned within him. Lyndon was not a bookish man who could spend his last years in reading and research. He was not a sportsman or hobbyist. He was under no pressure to make money; he already had millions. How *would* he live?

Before he left the White House he had decided on five major projects to complete the years just ahead. Together, they would enable him fully to occupy his time. As he flew back to Texas on Air Force One after the inauguration, he assembled his people around him—Mrs. Johnson, Walt Rostow, former White House speechwriters Bob Hardesty and Harry Middleton, former assistant press secretary Tom Johnson, his personal secretary Mary Rather—and outlined his plans. He wanted to build and staff the Lyndon B. Johnson School of Public Affairs at the University of Texas; he wanted to build and staff the Lyndon B. Johnson Presidential Library (also at the University); he wanted to see Mrs. Johnson's memoirs completed; he wanted to write his own book; and he wanted to prepare himself for a series of long interviews with Cronkite, which CBS would broadcast over a period of two or three years. For the interview and the books, the Johnsons were to be paid more than a million dollars.

These would be fairly demanding labors but it was still necessary to make the adjustment to Johnson City, Texas. He thought that could be accomplished, it seems, by transferring the habits developed governing a nation to the direction of these smaller affairs. He would, for example, rise early each morning—at 6 or 6:30 A.M.—and begin barking orders over the two-way radio network at the ranch. Instead of Rusk or McNamara or Valenti, the orders

went out to foremen and tractor operators and other members of his farm crews. He wanted to know how many eggs the chickens had laid, how the fertilizer was mixed, whether the tractor was operating as it should, whether the deer were being properly fed, whether this man or that was doing his job.

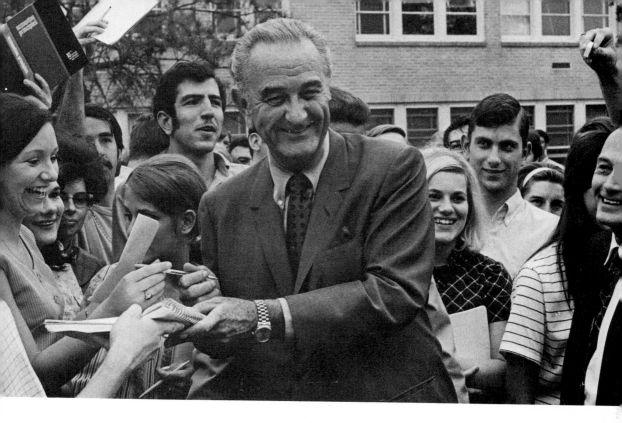

Lyndon often said he didn't want a "coat and tie" life after he retired, and at the ranch he didn't have one. But he always "dressed up" for his public appearances, particularly for his visits to young students. Those were the best times; he still relished the role of a teacher.

Beyond that, he retained some of the trappings of the White House. There were Secret Service agents around the ranch—three to a shift. Each morning an aide would drive in from Austin with the mail—3,000 letters a day in the first few months, 200 to 300 letters a day just before his death. Every Friday a courier, dispatched by President Nixon, flew down from Washington with a brief-case full of intelligence summaries on the war and other foreign affairs. Occasionally Richard Helms of the CIA or Army Chief of Staff William Westmoreland would go to the ranch to see him for a face-to-face briefing. There were frequent calls from the President, from Henry Kissinger, from Bob Haldeman. And the substantial staff of former White House aides who helped him on all of his projects, including the books, were available at all hours for conversation and companionship.

He always had had an appetite for luxury and size, and he continued to show these traits in his retirement years. In Austin, his powerful personal stamp was ever present: at the Federal Office Building, he maintained an office and staff; at his television station, another LBJ office and more secretaries; on the University of Texas campus, a third complement of secretaries and staff worked in yet another LBJ office in the Lyndon Baines Johnson Library (where there was also a replica of the White House Oval Office).

The library symbolized all these tendencies toward material extravagance. A few weeks after John Kennedy's assassination, he had said that he didn't intend to "build any libraries for myself." That was off-hand rhetoric, a slighting remark aimed at the Kennedys. Lyndon not only built a library for himself, he built the biggest, most expensive ($18.6 million) presidential library in the history of the Republic. It was eight stories tall and had a helicopter landing pad on the roof. Within its windowless walls of travertine marble, it housed 31 million papers, a collection more vast than the entire manuscript collection of the Library of Congress, a collection fifteen times larger than the one found in the Franklin Roosevelt library at Hyde Park. Critical visitors called it "Lyndon's Mausoleum" and compared it to the Great Pyramid at Giza. However that may be, it bore his clear imprint; it was a monument and, in an historical sense, was conceived as a vindication of his public life. "I want it all there [the record of his Administration] with the bark off," he said, "what I did right and what I did wrong."

His memoirs and the series of television interviews with Cronkite were to be forms of vindication, too, instruments for justifying his decisions and —not incidentally—for assigning blame for things that had gone wrong. These were to be the works of his last years as he cut himself off from public affairs to brood and think in that remote countryside so far from Washington, so far from power, so far from the troubles and triumphs he had known. On his first night at the ranch after leaving the White House, he later wrote,

I went out outside and stood in the yard again, looking up at the moon in the broad, clear Texas sky. My thoughts went back to that October night in 1957 when we had walked along the banks of the Perdenales River and looked for the Soviet Sputnik orbiting in the sky overhead. I thought of all that had happened in the years between. I remembered once again a story I had heard about one of the astronauts from the crew of Apollo 8, which a month ago had circled the moon only a few miles above its surface. Soon after his return to earth the astronaut had stepped into his backyard at home and had looked up at the moon. He had wondered if it really could be true that he had been there. I had recounted this story a few days ago to a group of friends. Perhaps, I told them, the time would come when I would look back on the majesty and the power and splendor of the Presidency and find it hard to believe that I had actually been there.

At the ranch, he had a sense of place. Despite all those years in Washington, despite all the travels throughout the world, his roots remained in Texas. He knew the families of his workers and the townspeople and the gullies and the streams and the places the deer grazed. He knew the names of his cattle and his horses: "They were his friends," one of his loyal employees has said, "he took an interest in them as he did in people." (Indeed, even in the White House he sometimes took what seemed to be an excessive interest in his animals. One day one of his dogs romping around the Oval Office relieved himself on the rug. Someone volunteered to clean up the mess, but Lyndon stopped him, bent over, and examined the fesces with a pencil, looking for worms.)

He was, as it turned out, at home in Texas and he adjusted to that environment far better than his wife had feared in 1964. He threw his great energies into ranching and his other projects as he had thrown them into his work in the Senate and in the presidency.

There was no lack of things to do, there was no problem filling up the days or the nights. In the evenings he would often surround himself with family and friends to watch movies (although he usually slept through them) or he would go visiting at the homes of friends like Arthur Krim, the movie magnate and Democratic money-raiser who had built a place on the lake near Lyndon's ranch. He had everything, it seemed. And yet he was denied what he wanted most: contentment. The knowledge that he was unloved and, by his own lights, unappreciated and misunderstood by his countrymen continued to haunt him. He still could not appear in public without the risk of insults and jeering. When his library was dedicated on the University of Texas campus in May, 1971, more than 3,000 dignitaries, led by President Nixon, took part. But even that ceremony was disrupted by protesters. They assembled nearby and tried to drown out the speakers with the cruel chants that damned him and "Johnson's war."

Opening Of The Great Pyramid Of Austin

©1971 HERBLOCK

He began smoking again, despite the warnings of his doctors. He ignored his diet and put on so much weight that television commentators remarked on it at the library dedication. The photographer Frank Wolfe once recorded a bantering scene in which Lady Bird scolded Lyndon about his diet. They were in his office in the Federal Building in Austin, and she caught him nibbling some cookies. As she admonished him, he praised her for her good figure and squeezed her leg in appreciation. They broke into laughter at his guile.

It was during these last years that he entered into a relationship with a young woman who, in many ways, symbolized those elements in American society that had come to despise him and his policies. Her name was Doris Kearns, and she was at the time a brilliant young assistant professor of government at Harvard University.

She had been born in Brooklyn of Roman Catholic parents, neither of whom had ever finished high school. Her academic record had gotten her scholarships and had launched her academic career—undergraduate work at Colby College in Maine and a doctoral degree from Harvard in 1966. In the mid-60s she got involved in the antiwar movement. In 1967 she was selected as one of the annual group of White House Fellows—promising young scholars who were given a year of practical experience working in Cabinet agencies or at the White House itself. Miss Kearns was then twenty-five.

The 1967 Fellows were invited to a White House reception on May 1. The President was there and he spotted Miss Kearns and danced with her several times. They talked about various things, and he remembered her two weeks later when an article appeared in the *New Republic* magazine entitled, "How to Remove LBJ in 1968." The authors were Doris Kearns and Sanford Levinson, a Harvard graduate student. Their thesis was simple: the "Left" should form a third party to ensure Johnson's defeat in 1968. His policies, they argued, had made "the American Dream a nightmare leading to *1984*."

The article caused a minor flurry at the White House and Miss Kearns was assigned to the Labor Department, rather than to the White House staff. Johnson did not forget her, however, and shortly after he had announced his decision not to seek re-election he had her transferred to his own staff.

In a later interview, she described the evolution of their relationship:

"What I think he really wanted was just somebody to talk to. When he would relax at night for an hour and a half, fairly frequently—a couple of times a week—I would go and talk to him. Or listen to him. He wanted an adversary. We would argue about the nature of the war. I would say, 'I know it's a civil war.' He would say, 'How the hell do you know that?' 'Well, I read Bernard Fall.' On the other hand, I was never convinced by him that it was a war of aggression. I'd say, 'How do you know?' (He would say) 'Well, the CIA says so.' That gap between our assumptions about the nature of the war was something the peace movement never came to grips with.

"He also talked to me for hours about his family. If I had known him at any other period, I don't think he'd ever have talked about things so reflectively . . . He's a man who needs and really thrives on talking with others. What we really became was friends, more than anything else."

She remained with Johnson as an assistant after her fellowship expired in the fall of 1968 and the following spring, after he had returned to the ranch, he asked her to help him with his book. She agreed and began a period of commuting between Harvard and Texas. She would spend days at a time with him, rewriting notes he would dictate to her for the book. In the mornings and sometimes at night they would swim in the pool at the ranch or take long walks and long drives.

They talked about many things besides politics. He would tell her about his life as a boy, about the stormy scenes between his parents, about the dreams that had bothered him all of his life. And he would question her about that strange academic world, populated with the intellectuals who had turned on him, had written savage denunciations of his policies, and had, in the end, helped pull him down.

Historians will explore this relationship in future years, as Miss Kearns may do in the book she plans to write one day. Whatever they conclude, it is necessary to understand the context in which their association flowered.

He was nearing the end of his life and she was young and intellectually exciting. Beyond that, she represented that Ivy League which "misunderstood" and reviled him and would, he feared, dismiss him with contempt in the histories and monographs that would pour out of the great Eastern universities. He may have seen her as a link to that alien world, as an instrument through which he could explain and justify himself and find, in time, the historical vindication he deeply desired. He would talk to her on this subject for hours in the monologue style we had gotten exposed to in those long sessions with him in Washington. In one of those conversations he told her:

"Fulbright and Mansfield believe you get peace by being soft and acting nice. But everything I know about history tells me that the only way to handle aggressors is to quarantine them like smallpox. All along it's been our lack of strength and our failure to show stamina that has gotten us into trouble. I was taught in high school and in college that we never would have gotten into World War I if the Kaiser hadn't believed he could count Uncle Sam out because our love of peace was being paraded so much. And I was taught in the Congress, by committees on defense preparedness and by FDR, that we were constantly telegraphing the wrong messages to Hitler and the Japs—that the Wheelers, the Lindberghs, the La Follettes and the America Firsters were letting Hitler know he could move without Uncle Sam. You see, we're up for grabs. We're the richest nation in the world. And when we look soft, the would-be aggressors go wild. It was the same thing in Korea and then in Laos.

"And now the same thing is happening again in Vietnam only this time it's World War III that is at stake. It was the worry of World War III that haunted me every night—even though I knew how long and drawn out the Vietnam war would be, even though I knew how unpopular it would be, even though I knew what it would do to my Great Society programs, still all the horror—as unbearable as it was—was acceptable if it prevented the far worse horror of World War III. For that would mean utter chaos—the loss of all control.

"It gives me goosebumps every time I hear the phrase 'no more Vietnams' because I fear we're entering a phase of withdrawal. And if that happens we'll lose all of Asia and then Europe and we'll be an island all to ourselves. And when all that comes to pass I'd sure hate to have to depend on the Galbraiths and that Harvard crowd to protect my property or lead me to the Burnet cave [a large cave near Austin]."

He was fully aware that she was part of "that Harvard crowd" and that awareness was crucial to him. "If I had been a young teacher at the University of Texas," Miss Kearns believes, "our relationship could never have happened. The fact that I was from Harvard was very important." She was plain-spoken, considerate of his views, and fascinated with him. But she was in no sense a prototype of the "Eastern Establishment." She was middle class, like Lyndon.

Lyndon's attempts to dominate the people around him are legendary. He would pick out clothes for his secretaries and send them up to New York to learn the secrets of makeup. He inquired intimately into their lives, lectured and sometimes bullied them about their personal habits and relationships. "He wanted," one of his intimate friends has said, "to possess people."

That seems to have occurred with Doris Kearns. When she was at the ranch he made constant demands on her time and attention. When she was away she says he would call her at all hours, sometimes demanding that she fly down to see him on the spur of the moment. He repeatedly told her, she has related, "I need you." He would tell her that she reminded him of his mother because of her intellectual interests and her strong will. She thinks he respected people who stood up to him and resisted his demands and recalls one such occasion. He insisted that she take a swim with him at the ranch one night and when she refused he said, admiringly, "You're an independent bitch!"

Inevitably, there were rumors and speculations about these two—an aging, declining man and a handsome young woman half his age. An item appeared in 1971 in *Parade Magazine* implying strongly that the relationship was more than platonic. Johnson was angered and so was his wife who blamed herself for bringing Miss Kearns to the ranch so often. Those who have known him and worked with him intimately for years—Jack Valenti, Tom Johnson, Horace Busby, Abe Fortas—insist it is inconceivable there was anything between them but friendship.

Again, the historians must ultimately resolve that question. For now, however, it is a fact that the relationship was real and close, that there is evidence it had begun the first time they met: "Didn't you feel what I felt?" he asked later. "Didn't you think it was something special?"

With Doris Kearns

Her own feelings, she has said, were always complex. She had great affection for Lyndon, he fascinated her, he impressed her. After all, he had been the President of the United States; she was a young girl out of Brooklyn, a young scholar privy to priceless insights into the mind and attitudes and psyche of one of the dominant figures of the age. In her view, her own feelings never progressed to romantic love. There were other men in her life. One of them, ironically, was Richard Goodwin, who had worked for John Kennedy and Lyndon Johnson and who had then abandoned Johnson to join happily in the effort to unseat him in 1968. (On the night of Johnson's withdrawal statement in March, 1968, Goodwin ran gleefully down the hall of a Milwaukee hotel where Eugene McCarthy was staying, shouting: "It only took six weeks to knock him out—only six weeks!")

There will always be speculations and imaginings about the role Doris Kearns played in the last years of Lyndon's life. We will never read his side of it. His associates of a lifetime disbelieve even the possibility of a romance. Indeed, some of these associates pleaded with us to omit any reference in this book to Doris Kearns. They argued, first, that any hint of a romantic relationship was untrue and, second, that it was unfair, in any case, to a dead man and his family. Further, they contended, there is no factual evidence to substantiate such a relationship. We do not purport to know the "truth" or all the ramifications of that relationship. There is, however, adequate evidence that she met some need in his life at that time, if only the need for companionship, for a sympathetic hearing, for help on the book. Some of her notes from those days are even now appearing in university circles on the East Coast. They contain valuable insights into his family relationships, his psychology, his dreams, his fears, and his disappointments.

One of those disappointments was the book on which he and Miss Kearns and others labored for months. It contained illuminating material on all the

major decisions of his presidency and was, in essence, a defense of his service to his country. But it sold poorly and received many critical and unsympathetic reviews. *The New York Times* critique was scathing:

Judging from its tepid language and its pop-magazine organization, the author was never even a tint more colorful than Calvin Coolidge. . . . Mr. Johnson treats his domestic program with justified pride. Yet so sappy is the language with which he describes its forging—so puffed up with bromides, platitudes and phrases such as "it had always grieved me greatly" . . . that its weight boils down to nothing.

There were other disappointments. Some of those who had been around him in the Senate and in the White House, people he had nurtured and given great responsibilities, had gone the way of Goodwin, Schlesinger, and others. Bill Moyers, whom he had regarded "almost like a son," George Reedy, McGeorge Bundy and, some would say, even McNamara.

And, finally, his body began to fail him, too. He was a sick man.

Americans had little impression of Lyndon during his retirement days. To all appearances he was living in the seclusion of his ranch, a largely silent figure from a dissonant, if recent, past. For a man who lived at the center of such intense public controversy, and who has never shirked battle, his last four years were marked by an uncharacteristic remoteness. He had little to say about the war or other events that had swirled around him. On rare occasions he would surface briefly, always inspiring a new ripple of controversy, and then again drop out of sight. He seemed deliberately to shun the publicity he had once courted so assiduously in times of his peak popularity and received so relentlessly when the public turned against him.

The first indication that his health might be failing came on March 2, 1970, slightly more than a year after he left the White House. He was stricken at the ranch and flown immediately to Brooke General Hospital, an Army installation in San Antonio, suffering chest pains. Lyndon recovered; it had not seemed serious.

A month later, after his discharge from the hospital, he came back to Washington for the first time as a private citizen. It was the last time we saw Lyndon Johnson. He came to lunch at the *Washington Post* that Tuesday, April 7, 1970. Some five hours later he left us all drained, fascinated, enthralled, and full of questions that never could be answered or resolved. Probably none of us present that day could successfully capture or reconstruct all the moods, the picturesque language, the mobile expressions, or the specific points he made. It was, at the least, a virtuoso performance. He was soft, sarcastic, crisp, commanding, anecdotal, colorful—and in the end confounding as always.

Lyndon was telling us his story, and speaking to his place in history. He was a salesman, and he came prepared with the goods in the form of stacks of papers marked TOP SECRET and TOP SECRET SENSITIVE. Over and over, he read from the various memoranda, letters, and other documents to back up his positions. He would snap his fingers and command his silent young aide, Tom Johnson, to produce this paper and that document and that letter and that memo.

In retrospect, what was most memorable about his performance was not what he said about the war or his critics or other aspects of his presidency. It was the two sides of Lyndon Johnson displayed that made the most lasting impression. A subdued, somber Lyndon first appeared. His initial conversation was all about his health and recent hospitalization. He had aged dramatically.

"He came in a little after 12:30," one of us wrote immediately after the long luncheon, looking less tall, less bulky than I had remembered. His hair was almost completely white and was growing long in the back in the old-fashioned Southern senator style, the way Mendel Rivers wears it. His illness showed in his face, I thought, and from the side his skin had the yellowish-gray look you find on extremely sick men. His hands were mottled with crimson splotches; there was a scab on the back of one finger and lots of freckles, all of which brought images of an old man.

Lyndon's manner reinforced the impression. He seemed tired, withdrawn, quiet, and preoccupied with problems of his health. He was on a diet of 850 calories a day, he said, and was getting back his strength gradually. There had been quite a bit of pain this time, he said. It was much more serious than the public knew. His trouble really had begun the previous spring when he was working on his ranch. He liked to get out and take his exercise, he went on slowly. One day he was laying lengths of pipe, lifting and placing them in the mud. Suddenly he became short of breath and began to experience slight pains in his chest. He remembered stopping his work without quite realizing why.

For the next hour at the luncheon he continued in the same vein. He was the old statesman, above partisanship. There was none of the remembered Johnson fire and flash, none of the earthy anecdotes about men and events. He preferred to speak philosophically, it seemed, to talk about the memoirs on which he was working each day, to reflect on the higher problems of the presidency (he favored a single six-year term, and he didn't think being a lame-duck President necessarily reduced a chief executive's power).

But gradually his manner and mood changed. He began talking about Vietnam, and suddenly he was more vigorous and assertive. He folded and unfolded his napkin, began leaning forward, rocking back and forth in his chair, speaking first slowly and then loudly. Now he was, clearly, LBJ. To quote another of the many recollections we composed that day:

As he talked he seemed to take on another appearance. The pallor and signs of sickness went away and all of a sudden you were sitting with a vigorous, commanding, strong man whose mind was so clear, so well organized, so quick, that you instantly became aware of the power of his personality, of the ability to dominate and persuade and overwhelm.

Lyndon gave us a detailed chronology of the steps that led him to announce the bombing halt and of his own decision to renounce the presidency on March 31, 1968. That decision, he said, was prompted by a "noble reason": he wanted to serve his country. He introduced his subject in typical fashion: "Now, I don't want you good people to have a heart attack here at this good table eating this good food. And if any of you has heart trouble, you better take nitroglycerine now, because the first person to urge me to halt the bombing was Walt Rostow. That was in May of 1967. Two weeks later the same proposal was made by McNamara." McNamara repeated the proposal in a formal memo dated November 1, 1967. Lyndon held it up and read from it.

He then launched into a day-by-day account of the events as they unfolded in that critical time of decision during March of 1968. He recalled incidents down to the precise minute they occurred: "At 8:44 A.M. I . . . " and at "4:45 P.M. I went into my bedroom and stripped off my clothes to get some rest" and at "8:30 P.M. I went into the bathroom to comb my hair and fix my tie, and when I walked out I handed Clark Clifford and Walt Rostow the speech I was going to give. I told them I thought they'd be particularly interested in the first part and in the last two pages. They might find that part especially interesting." It contained his statement saying he was not going to be a candidate for President.

He spelled out, in the same minute detail, the sequence of events: how on March 4 Dean Rusk sent him a proposal urging that consideration be given to halting the bombing and making a move for peace that was relayed to Rusk, through the British Ambassador, from British Foreign Secretary George Brown; how the task force reports from the military recommended 205,000 additional troops for Vietnam with the dispatch of 22,000 more immediately and that a reserve call-up of 262,000 plus increased draft support be implemented, all of which would cost some 8 to 10 billion dollars more; how the debate continued and who said what to whom and at what moment, and how finally Lyndon told his advisers: "Get on your horses and get me a plan." (He also said, "If you call up the Reserves all you're going to get is a lot of pot bellies.")

Perhaps the most fascinating—and contradictory—part of the LBJ scenario came when he described what happened on March 20th. He began that day with a private meeting with his new Secretary of Defense, Clark Clifford, he said, and then he gave a command to Tom Johnson and soon was holding a folder marked "Clifford." He read us from the summation of his remarks to Clifford.

They were speaking, he said, about the speech he planned to make at the end of the month on the war. Lyndon said he told Clifford:

"I am going to be the peace candidate."

We must have, he said he told Clifford, "a Churchill peace, not a Chamberlain peace. We must win the peace, not the way the Athenians won it, but the way that Harry Truman won it with Greece and Turkey." We must have a new approach to show we mean to take a new direction. "I've got to get me a peace proposal."

By then the draft of his March 31 speech already contained a proposal for a partial bombing halt. But later that afternoon, when meeting again with his advisers, Lyndon said he told them: "Get that peace out of there!" "I'll deal with that later if I decide to do so," he said.

At this point, noting our incredulous expressions around the dining table, Lyndon stopped, laughed, and then remarked that this was an indication of just how "complex" a character he was. It was then that, tapping his forehead, he said: "Sometimes even I don't know what's going on up there."

That was a confounding enough statement, but what he had said to prompt our reaction was even more confounding. For March 20th was only four days after Robert Kennedy had announced his presidential candidacy and eight days after Eugene McCarthy's surprisingly strong showing in the New Hampshire primary. Lyndon had already told, earlier in the luncheon, how he had never wanted to be President, and had recounted one more time the story of Bird talking him out of turning down the 1964 nomination. Now, here he was, saying he wanted to be known as "the peace candidate" only eleven days before he finally renounced the presidency. Did he, then, really want the 1968 nomination after all? And was he thinking of turning the tables on the McCarthy-Kennedy candidacies by becoming the *real* peace candidate? Did he secretly harbor, even after his March 31 speech, the wish that he be "drafted" by the Democrats at Chicago that coming summer? Did he himself really know what he wanted? Who can say? He did tell us that up until 9 o'clock on the night he spoke to the country he hadn't completely made up his mind. He might have deleted his withdrawal statement if Westmoreland had disagreed with his plan or if Robert Kennedy had attacked him.

Lyndon also demonstrated another aspect of his complexities that day. He clearly showed how he liked to work in the utmost secrecy, even to the point of keeping things away from his closest Cabinet officers. Those who are writing about what happened in his Administration, he said, have seen "only a fragment" of what took place. No one won any battle for his mind. He told how Dean Rusk habitually would not express his true convictions or real feelings at a Cabinet meeting or a top-level security session or even at the most private "Tuesday luncheon" groups that Lyndon held every week with his most trusted and valued advisors. After a meeting would break up, he said, Rusk would say, "Mr. President, may I see you a second about another matter?" Often, the two men would walk into "the bedroom" or some other place; then, and only then, Rusk would say what he truly thought.

In the same way, Lyndon himself described how he would ask a key aide for his private advice and then float the suggestions among other principal counselors. Thus, each was left thinking he alone had offered the President his private counsel. Lyndon told, for instance, of circulating a memo from, say, Clifford to McNamara and Katzenbach and Rusk without informing any of them who had advocated what. The same was true of men like Arthur Goldberg, who also had urged him to change his Vietnam policies in March of 1968. Lyndon also showed how distrustful he was of key elements in the government. At the Pentagon, he said, darkly, there was a group that was out to do him in, a group that regularly "leaked" information to the *Post* and the *New York Times*. He didn't want to categorize or name them, but they came in with McNamara. Though he didn't say it—and didn't have to—they were obviously the "Kennedy men." He described them, disparagingly, as holding an "Eastern huddle." During the most delicate maneuvers late in his presidency, he said, he often sent cables that were not even seen by the Pentagon. They were dispatched through "back channels," presumably the CIA network. He recalled that once Rusk told him that Clifford "has to be brought in on this." His resentment at men who had served and left him also came out vividly. When Clifford took over in the Pentagon from McNamara, he said, Clifford searched for a certain key document dealing with Vietnam. It was missing. "Maybe McNamara stole it and took it away overnight," Lyndon said.

Even the man he seems to have trusted the most at the end—Rusk—did not escape an occasional presidential tirade. Only Rusk knew fully what his plans for the bombing halt were that March, he told us. Then, on the afternoon of March 23 (it was 4 P.M., he said, again delighting in demonstrating his memory) he had put on his pajamas and started to nap in the White House. He had just prepared for bed when Harry McPherson came to him with a proposal for a partial bombing halt. Lyndon was shocked, and then furious. He thought Rusk, the only one who knew what he was considering, was lobbying privately with White House advisers. He feared a "leak." Immediately, Lyndon called Rusk. The Secretary was home, sick, but Lyndon got him anyway, and sharply upbraided him. "I said some things I shouldn't have said," he reported. Rusk assured him he had not violated the confidence; he had informed only one man, who helped draft cables, and he was certain the man was trustworthy. Lyndon asked Rusk for the record.

In our conversation, Lyndon disparaged his critics and political enemies, though not in the crushing fashion he sometimes employed. He was particularly sensitive, and resentful, about government officials who were beginning to tell their versions of events in public. They didn't know what had happened. Townsend Hoopes, the Pentagon official who had written critically of Lyndon's presidency, "had only been to the White House five times—twice in the basement, once at a Medal of Honor ceremony. . . . Why, I wouldn't know the man if he walked in the door." At another point he said: "It's not important if I saw Kay Graham going to the ladies room on my way to a decision. It's the decision that counts."

His old love-hate relationship with the press still figured strongly in his words. At some length, he said he agreed with many of Spiro Agnew's criticisms of the monopolistic liberalism of the Eastern press. He wanted the press to police itself, to establish some standards of performance that some kind of an editors' committee might monitor. If that isn't done, he suggested, the government might erode the First Amendment. Frank Stanton and Kay Graham and Lady Bird don't control the media; the media had become vehicles for the opinions of "some young college students," "some 17-year-old" who gets on the air to espouse "McCarthy" and "Mark Rudd" points of view.

He had written these thoughts about the press in an article for *The Reader's Digest*, but decided to delete them. "I didn't want to seem to be a Junior Agnew."

He was also disturbed about the direction the Supreme Court seemed to be taking. Abe Fortas's departure from the court had hurt the country. He had hoped that with Fortas and later perhaps men like Homer Thornberry and Cyrus Vance on the court America could be assured of the highest quality of judicial representation. The court situation was, in his mind, linked to the political directions of the country. Lyndon was afraid the nation was still divided. Although he didn't spell it out precisely, he seemed to fear that the country was going through one of its retrogressive periods similar to that of Harding, Coolidge, and Hoover following Wilson. What worried him most was the thought that there could be real repression growing out of extreme polarization between left and right.

The most fascinating thing about Lyndon that day was not what he said specifically about Vietnam or any topics, but how he said it. He was overpowering. He thumped on the table, moved back and forth vigorously, grimaced, licked his lips, gestured with his arms, slumped back into his seat, switched from a sharp to a soft story, and kept the conversation going from the moment he sat down at the dining table until hours later when Lady Bird called the *Post* and sent in a note reminding him he should come home and rest.

As he reminisced, going back into his childhood and then on through his entire political career, he became more colloquial and more Texan. His daddy used to whip him with a razor strop, he said, and "It hurt him more than it hurt me. But that's the kind of thing you have to do in a family." In a way, it was the same as being President: there were certain things you had to do that were unpopular, but you did them for the public benefit.

His language, and phrases, were picturesque:

"So I took a cold belly buster . . . "

"Anyone who's smart enough to pour piss from a boot . . . "

"And Dick Russell said, 'I've been to the duck blind with the man. I know him. I may not agree with him on everything, but he's a good man, he cares for the people, and he'll try to do what's right [referring to his plans to nominate his friend, Judge Homer Thornberry of Texas, to the Supreme Court].' "

"Those Laotians can't stop anybody. They just stand around throwing water at each other."

"MacArthur pinned a medal on me for heroism. It looks good on my chest" —here, he fingered the Silver Star citation in his coat lapel—"but it's a good thing they couldn't see what that flight did to my pants."

He recalled a story from his early days as a young Texas congressman. Elliott Roosevelt, the President's son, came to him on behalf of electrical power interests in Texas, he said. This was at a time when Lyndon was fighting the power companies there.

"I always liked Elliott," he said. "He was a good boy. But they'd got to him, and so he came down there to see me and asked me to ease up on them. He said he had talked with his daddy and his daddy wanted him to tell me that he agreed. So I said, 'All right, I'll do that, Elliott. But before I do, I want you to do one thing for me. I want you to go back to your daddy and tell him I'll do it if he wants me to, but ask him to write me a letter, in his own hand, saying what he wants, and then sign it.' Well, I could see Elliott wasn't expecting that. I'd kind of roughed him up. So he said, 'Why do you want Father to write you a letter? I've already seen him, and he wants you to do this.' And I told him, 'Well, Elliott, it's this way: when I do what your daddy wants and I come back to Texas they're going to run me out of the state. Now the nearest border is 150 miles away and that's over the bridge to Mexico. And I figure I can get to that bridge before they get me, and when I'm half way over, and on the Mexican side, I want to be able to turn around and stop and hold up that letter showing the signature of Franklin Delano Roosevelt so everyone can read it. Like this.' "

He held up an imaginary piece of paper, relishing the role he was playing and the laughter it inspired.

Lyndon was full of such performances. He acted out various roles. He mimicked people: Clark Clifford sitting up straight and dignified like this (he sat up very straight and very solemnly in his chair and folded his arms over his chest); Hubert Humphrey and HHH's reaction to the news LBJ was going to renounce the presidency in 1968: "I told him not to go off to Mexico, but I guess he didn't believe me." Lyndon gave a "hee-hee-hee-hee-hee" rendition to show how silly Humphrey thought the idea.

As he looked back on his presidency, he became more serious and philosophical. He obviously took great pride in the domestic achievements during his time as President. (He used the term, "my 2,000 days in the White House." He was going to top Kennedy to the end.) He told, in loving detail, how many bills had passed, and how long those acts would endure, and how they would improve the health and education and environment of Americans not yet born. "Now you take education," he said. "I remember Homer Ferguson arguing over appropriating $400,000 for education. It was subversive and socialistic. And I got through billions for education as President." He still deeply believed in the Great Society, and told a story to make his point: There was a preacher who came to the White House, and he gave a great sermon, ringing with conviction and eloquence as he appealed for social justice. Throughout the sermon, Maurice Stans, later to be the Republican financial chief of Richard Nixon's Committee for the Re-election of the President, was sitting there nodding silently, and Stans, said Lyndon, had "only one thought in his mind, 'How much will it cost?' "

As for his own place in history, Lyndon seemed content to wait. He seemed to have no doubts about what he had achieved for the country at home. But the war in Vietnam obviously had left him baffled about the attitudes of Americans—and it had hurt him because he knew the war had obscured the works of his Great Society. Interestingly, he said he was not at all sure, now in his retirement reflections, that he had been right about Vietnam—but for a different reason than you might think. He wondered if history wouldn't judge him more harshly for not being more aggressive in that war, for not deciding either to go in all the way, or get out, but mainly for not going in to win, and win quickly. He wondered if he had been right in his March 31 decision about the Vietnam de-escalation process that was followed by Nixon. He wasn't at all sure.

Finally, after nearly five hours, when Lady Bird's note was sent into the dining room asking him to come home, Lyndon said to us, beginning his farewells, "I want you to know no matter how we differ about things, I feel I am at the table of friends, and I want to thank you for letting me come and visit with you."

Here he was, he went on, in the twilight of his years, among good friends. Three men had been most influential in his life, he said: his daddy, Franklin Roosevelt, "who was like a daddy to me," and Phil Graham, the late publisher of the *Washington Post*. "Phil used to abuse me and rail at me and tell me what was wrong with me," Lyndon recalled, "and just when I was ready to hit him, he'd laugh in that way of his to let me know he loved me. And he made me a better man." Kay Graham knew, he said, turning to Mrs. Graham seated next to him and touching her arm fondly, that a great deal of what later became the Great Society was written out at Phil's farm in Virginia in 1960 before Lyndon became Vice-President. Those were good days.

He had one more story to tell. It was a story Sam Rayburn used to tell about a small Texas town. Once, when Rayburn was just beginning as a politician, everyone important in that town had turned him down when he was looking for a place to spend the night—the banker, the newspaper editor, the judge. Finally a little old blacksmith said he would be glad to take Rayburn in for the night. Years later, after Rayburn had become famous and powerful, he came back to that town. Everyone clamored for him, the banker, the newspaper editor, the judge. They all wanted the honor of his staying with them. No, Rayburn told each to his face, he didn't want to stay with them. But was that little old blacksmith still there? Yes, he was. Bring him to me, Rayburn commanded. When the blacksmith came, Rayburn told him: "Jeeter, I'd like to spend the night at your house if you'll have me." The blacksmith did, and kept Rayburn up half the night talking. When Rayburn said he had to go to sleep, for he had a busy day ahead of him, tears welled up in the blacksmith's eyes.

"Mr. Sam, I'd just like to talk to you all night."

And that, Lyndon Baines Johnson said, was the way he felt about his friends at the *Post*.

There were some bitter-end Johnson critics among those of us around that dining table, but when Lyndon stood up to begin shaking each person's hand to say good-bye we all spontaneously burst into applause. Some of us had tears in our eyes.

We thought we might never see his likes again. And perhaps we were right.

Exactly one year to the day after his *Post* luncheon—April 7, 1972—Lyndon suffered a heart attack while visiting his older daughter, Lynda, and son-in-law, Charles (Chuck) Robb, at their home in Farmington, Virginia, about three miles from the University of Virginia campus in Charlottesville. He was stricken at 4 o'clock in the morning and immediately taken to the University hospital. He stayed in the hospital only five days, and then returned to the ranch to recuperate. It had not seemed, in the public reports at that time, to have been a critical blow, but it was. He was failing now. After his death a heart specialist who treated him in Charlottesville said the 1972 attack had been as massive as the one in 1955. For the rest of his days, he experienced sharp pains in his chest that indicated his heart muscle was not getting enough blood. Although the general public was not aware of his true condition, Lyndon himself, his friends insist, knew he was dying.

He immediately began setting his house in order. He was determined to leave his wife and family in the best possible financial condition, and he personally negotiated the sale of fixed assets—the television station in Austin, the ranch land, and other properties. His estate, he knew, was in superb shape.

Lyndon's health continued to worsen. That fall, he privately consulted Dr. Michael De Bakey, a noted Texas heart surgeon, about the possibility of an operation. Given his condition, the risk of cardiac surgery was too great. He not only had severe heart disease, but he was afflicted with what the doctors later said was "extensive diverticulosis of the colon." In those last months he had several severe attacks of diverticulitis.

He made one last major public appearance. On December 12, 1972, civil rights leaders from across the country, both black and white, gathered at the Lyndon B. Johnson Library in Austin for a symposium. The occasion was the opening of Lyndon's presidential civil rights papers, some million in all. The symposium brought together many of those associated with the glory days of the civil rights era of the '60s: Earl Warren, Roy Wilkins, Hubert Humphrey, Burke Marshall, Clarence Mitchell. An ice storm had hit the area, making travel hazardous, and Lyndon was feeling "poorly." His doctors advised him not to make the speech he had planned, he told the audience, but "I'm going to speak anyway because I've got something I want to say."

Many of Lyndon's friends and associates have said it was a shame that the American public never saw the real man. His speeches—particularly the presidential television addresses—and his book never reflected his mercurial, anecdotal qualities. For the most part, he came over as wooden and labored. Little of the Lyndon we had listened to in private ever emerged. This time in Austin, though, it was different. Lyndon was both colloquial and eloquent. His remarks were studded with such expressions as "To be black in a white society is not to stand on level and equal ground." And: "Now, let me make it plain that when I say 'black'—as I do a good many times in this little statement—I also mean brown and yellow and red and all other people who suffer discrimination because of their color or their heritage."

For once before the TV cameras and a large audience, he was not reluctant to be Lyndon, the Texas story teller.

"I have served with many Presidents and I think I have a viewpoint that no other person in this room has about the presidency," he said. "Out in my little town one time, where court week is very exciting, all the boys would leave town to avoid the grand jury, and all the citizens would go to court to hear the proceedings. The town drunk came up to the hotel one morning as the old judge was leaving and said, 'Would you give a poor man a dime for a cup of coffee?' And the judge said, 'Hell, no. Get out of the way. I wouldn't give a tramp anything.' And the poor fellow with a hangover—some of you wouldn't understand that [loud laughter this time]—walked off the porch dejectedly. And just as he got to the end of the porch the judge said, 'Come back. If you'd like to have a quarter for a pick-me-up, I'd be glad to help you.' [Again, he was interrupted by laughter.] And he handed the old fellow a quarter. Then he looked up at him, startled but with great appreciation in his eyes, and said, 'Judge, you've been there, haven't you?' "

The laughter was louder this time. While he was telling that story, Lyndon paused briefly at one point and unobtrusively raised his hand to his mouth. He was having chest pains again, and he took nitroglycerin to ease the pains. Later, in his last interview with Walter Cronkite, he told how "I just stopped and calmly pulled out a little nitroglycerin and took it right in front of the thousands—I guess they got it on television. But it didn't bother me. As soon as I got a little relief from it, I went on."

He finished his speech on a serious note, one that evoked the days when he had resolved the Selma crisis: "We have proved that great progress is possible. We know how much still remains to be done. And if our efforts continue, and if our will is strong, and if our hearts are right, and if courage remains our constant companion, then, my fellow Americans, I am confident we shall overcome."

Even then, in his last public appearance, Lyndon was to hear the sound of dissent and disunity. As soon as he had completed his address, two blacks—Roy Innis, of the Congress of Racial Equality, and the Reverend Kendall Smith of New York—took the podium to deliver unscheduled speeches. The conference, they protested, did not include speakers holding other than "Establishment" views. They urged those present to pass resolutions calling for more aggressive action, and to schedule a follow-up meeting. But this time Lyndon was strongly defended.

Clarence Mitchell, a black, and the Washington director of the NAACP, rose in the audience to say:

"I knew—when I saw Roy walk in there and I saw the deployment of his forces—what was going to happen because I have been through this before and it is only out of the courtesy of a great President of the United States that this gentleman has had an opportunity to be heard. It seems to me this is what is the challenge of leadership. If President Johnson had the courage to come up in Texas and speak against white demagoguery, wherever I am I'm going to come out and speak against black demagoguery."

Lyndon, who had been sitting in the audience listening intently, came back to the rostrum. He walked slowly, and with obvious effort. He appeared drawn and fatigued. He waved away Reverend Smith, who walked off murmuring apologies. Then, once more, he took the microphone. Lyndon, to the end a politician who believed that people should reason together, was conciliatory. He agreed with the dissidents, and urged them to meet with President Nixon to press their grievances.

"I think you should try to reason with the President," he said. "There's nothing wrong with asking for an hour of his time. You don't have to start off telling him he's terrible. He doesn't think he is. He doesn't want to leave the White House feeling he has been unjust."

That was Lyndon's last speech and fittingly, in extemporaneous fashion, it summed up the lessons of his entire political career. Six weeks later it was January 20th again, another inauguration day, and now Americans were awaiting news they hoped their President would give them: that the war in Vietnam was finally over.

Lyndon was not in Washington. At the very time the nation was watching President Nixon take the oath of office on the Capitol steps, Lyndon was helping Lady Bird plant trees along a road that links the ranch with a state park. Only about six spectators watched as they planted the first of 100 redbuds that will grace the area he loved.

Two days later, at 3:50 P.M. on Monday, January 22, 1973, Lyndon reached for a phone in his bedroom at the ranch and asked for the head of his Secret Service detail. The agent was in a car at the time; another man answered the call. Lyndon asked him to come immediately to the bedroom. He did not say why. When the agents arrived, they found the 36th President of the United States lying on the floor next to his bed, apparently dead.

His death came quietly, in lonely seclusion, after a stormy life played out largely in public view. His wife, who had stood by him in every crisis and on whom he relied so much, was away. His daughters, grandchildren, friends, and cronies whom he loved to regale with his inimitable stories were absent.

Lyndon Baines Johnson, that most public man, who was in his element when surrounded by cheering crowds, had died alone, calling for help.

Lyndon: An Appraisal

Not long after he became President, Lyndon took a reporter on a tour of his ranch. He pointed out the bluebonnets and the cattle and the rolling hill country, and then escorted him a mile or so away to the small house where he was born. There, in the shade of a grove of live oak trees near the Pedernales River, he showed the graves of his grandparents and his mother and father. Then, waving toward a particularly handsome and large live oak, he said: "And that's where I'm going to be buried, right there under that tree."

Shortly before his death Lyndon asked Billy Graham, the evangelist, to come see him at the ranch. He took Graham to the same site and told him: "One day you are going to be asked to preach at my funeral. You'll come right here under this tree and I'll be buried right there. You'll preach the Bible and preach the gospel and I want you to. I hope you'll tell people about some of the things I tried to do."

Lyndon's wishes were observed, of course, and his funeral was carried out, as he had instructed, in both grand and simple fashion. It was, appropriately, an event in which the old and the new were inextricably intertwined. Americans seemed to feel a sadness at the timing and manner of his passing. It was as if Lyndon achieved in death what he sought and could not accomplish in life—a time of national healing and reconciliation—for the day after he died, Richard Nixon announced the final cease-fire agreement in Vietnam. The war with which Lyndon always will be associated was coming to an end, at least for Americans, and there was a rush of hope that the rancor and bitterness that had so divided the nation for a decade would also subside. His funeral became one of those rare moments when national mourning was combined with a sense of a nation beginning anew.

In a way, everyone who spoke about him expressed those thoughts. They

urged their countrymen to see Lyndon in a larger light.

There was Dean Rusk, standing in the cold, stone space of the Capitol rotunda with a bright winter sun filtering through the skylight in the dome, facing the flag-covered casket and surrounded by those who had once followed Lyndon loyally and opposed him bitterly, saying: "Today's writers are inclined to discuss Lyndon Johnson almost solely in terms of Vietnam with such questions as whether he did too much or too little in that tragic struggle. The historians will take a broader view." Recalling Lyndon's last State of the Union address and reciting the last sentence, "But I believe that at least it will be said that we tried," Rusk added: "Ah, yes, he tried, with reckless disregard to his own life."

There was Jake Pickle, the Congressman from the hill country in Texas, speaking in such familiar Southwestern accents and in such a homespun manner that it seemed as if Lyndon himself were delivering the funeral oration. At the end of his eulogy, Pickle's voice broke and he was near tears as he concluded: "The President will rest in his beloved hill country where he has told us his father before him said he wanted to be—home, 'where folks know when you're sick and care when you die.' " There he paused, his voice cracking, before saying: "Two hundred million Americans care, Mr. President. We care —and we love you."

There was evidence that many Americans, many no doubt with a strong sense of surprise, found they did care: At Andrews Air Force base, where the Johnson plane landed bringing the body back to Washington, the same plane in which Lyndon had become President on that day in Dallas a decade before, a black sergeant carrying the coffin moved slowly forward in the bright sunshine with tears streaking his face. At Constitution Avenue on the way to the Capitol where the crowds were massed five and six deep and were marked by a deep and respectful silence, a construction worker stood at attention as the caisson bearing the coffin passed by, his white hard hat over his heart. At the church on Thomas Circle, as the honor guard slowly brought in the casket to place it on the red velvet catafalque before the altar, women reached for their handkerchiefs and men wiped their eyes. At the grave, under the live oak branches, more tears and muffled sobs as the pasture land was crowded with the famous and mighty of the country along with the ordinary people of Texas all standing together in the mud paying their last respects to one of the most tempestuous Presidents in our history. Lyndon would have liked it that Ethel Kennedy, Bobby's widow, was there, and she was crying too.

In the outpouring of reminiscences and instant appraisals that inevitably follow the passing of a powerful and controversial figure, there were exaggerated claims of greatness and nobility for him in death that were just as exaggerated as the venomous remarks about him had been in life. All this will change, and Lyndon some day will find his rightful place in history's verdict.

James MacGregor Burns, a distinguished historian and biographer of both Franklin Roosevelt and John Kennedy, has said that history "has a way of siphoning into oblivion the petty and the irrelevant and of measuring up the real stature of a man." Burns wrote in a testimonial volume presented to the President in 1969:

Some historians will remember Lyndon B. Johnson as the man who declared total war on poverty, deprivation, disease, and ignorance—and who threw himself, day and night, into the leadership of that battle with every ounce of energy he possessed. Other historians will remember him as the man who—like Jackson and Wilson and Truman—suffered criticism because he stuck to the course that he believed was right; a man who endured attacks with the patience and tolerance of a Lincoln; and as a man who risked the consensus he cherished because he put duty and conscience over an easy popularity. Still other historians will remember him as the man from the South and from the Senate who made a personal and political commitment to full opportunity for black Americans—a commitment that stamped him as truly the President of all the people and a symbol of hope for the whole nation.

Students of government, like myself, will remember Lyndon Johnson for a further and special reason. He was the first President to recognize fully that our basic social ills are so rooted in encrusted attitudes and stubborn social structures that no single solution or dramatic crusade will solve them: the first President to see clearly that only a total attack across the widest front, with every possible weapon, would bring a break-through; and the first President to propose basic institutional changes to make a total attack possible. No one defined the problem better than the President himself: "Our democracy cannot remain static, a prisoner to the past. . . . Government itself has the continuing obligation—second to no other—to keep the machinery of public participation functioning smoothly and to improve it where necessary so that democracy remains a vital and vibrant institution."

Our own view, of necessity, is limited. In the popular picture, partly self drawn, partly cruel caricature, Lyndon was a monumental egotist with an unbridled passion for power and place. We saw him as something else—as a man of massive talent, and equally massive insecurities. Looking back on it now, everything he did seemed to fit the pattern. Lyndon didn't just want a *good* society, in the term cast by Walter Lippmann in the 1930s; he wanted a *great* society. He didn't want to equal his mentor, Franklin Roosevelt; he wanted to eclipse him. He didn't want just to rebuild Southeast Asia; he wanted to transform it into a grander Europe. He was contradictory, complex, confounding. He could be cruel and vindictive, kind and thoughtful. He could be sentimental and weep in public—and did on the day Roosevelt died. He could be vulgar, petty, scheming, conspiratorial—and compassionate and generous. We will not forget him.

His very initials were so much a mark of the man. The LBJ Ranch, Lady Bird Johnson, Lynda Bird Johnson, Luci Baines Johnson. He even named one of his dogs Little Beagle Johnson. It was proof, if any more were needed, that Lyndon needed to leave his mark. Some saw this as a sinister manifestation of a deeper psychological problem: he was so vainglorious, so absorbed in himself, that he could not distinguish issues clearly. Everything came through colored by the complexities of his personality.

But Lyndon was more than a victim of himself—of his excesses, his flamboyance, his manner and style, his penchant for secrecy and manipulation, his tall tales and outright lies, of the public impression he helped create of himself as a Machiavellian politician, the master of the deal, the biggest political operator of them all. In a larger sense he was also a victim of circumstances over which he had no control—of the aura of the young and elegant President who had been assassinated, of the resentment of those who were waiting for a Kennedy restoration, of prejudice toward Southerners, of arrogance on the part of the intellectuals whose approval he so desperately wanted, of the policies of the past that he did not fashion, of the lack of public appreciation for the role of a politician, its limitations and possibilities

After Lyndon's death, Dean Rusk spoke of the problems of "the politics of the Southern accent." Rusk meant, as he expressed the thought: "Now, there are places in our country which will accept any accent in the world—German, Oxford, Russian, Yiddish—but not a Southern accent, because they think that anyone with a Southern accent somehow is a little stupid. Now, one of the things that is going to surprise the historians when they get full access to those 31 million documents in the Johnson Library will be the intellectual power of this man. But this was concealed from some elements in our society by his Southern accents and his homely and cornpone stories."

That is too simple a judgment. Lyndon's problems in the presidency transcended his accent and mannerisms, his origins and his personality. His hero, Franklin Roosevelt, had come to power in the 1930s when certain fundamental ideas about the nature of government and society and America's role in the world were approaching full tide. One of those ideas involved the perfectibility of man and society. It was the optimistic belief that rational men making rational choices could create, through government action, a society of justice, harmony, and tranquility—all within the structure of a capitalist economy. The other great idea of that period was that the United States had a holy mission in the world, to be the "arsenal of democracy," the ultimate shield against totalitarianism.

Johnson inherited those beliefs. A "Great Society," he naively insisted, could be created through government fiat, through the process of "reasoning together" and through relatively minor alterations in the system—aid to education, manpower training, and similar ameliorative measures. He accepted, too, the concept of America's "mission" in the world as the last defense against "aggression "

Let it be said that he was not alone. These were the beliefs of John Kennedy, they were the beliefs of the liberals in his own party, of that "Eastern crowd" he both envied and feared. It was one of the ironies that marked his life that the intellectual foundations of the New Deal (which he accepted) and the intellectual foundations of America's postwar foreign policy (which he also accepted) were being eroded and discredited even as he took office.

As the revisionist critiques took hold, it was easy enough for many men to change their views—to decide, for example, that no "vital American interests" were at stake in Vietnam. But Lyndon had made decisions based on the old assumptions. He had launched his "war on poverty" and had committed billions to it. He had sent all those boys—hundreds of thousands—into Vietnam.

He could not undo what he had done. The dice had been rolled; the commitments had been made. He was truly like Macbeth in that respect, trapped by the terrible knowledge that "going back is more tedious than going o'er." He had carried the philosophy and ideals of the New Dealers to their logical limits at the very time that the tide was running out on all their premises and assumptions.

In that sense, his tragedy, above all, was a tragedy arising out of the best liberal impulses of his own generation and of a younger generation symbolized at the beginning of the '60s by the Kennedys. And it was not his tragedy alone, although he became the scapegoat for it in the minds and writings of transient critics. It was genuinely an American tragedy, in which the selfless and soaring desire to perform good works in the world became corrupted with that arrogance of pride the Greeks called *hubris*. In the end, of course, the arrogance and simplistic idealism were swept away on that tide of events he had dimly anticipated early in his term before these grand adventures, including Vietnam, were launched.

We think that for all the bitterness his presence engendered, for all the anger and outrage that swirled around his time in office, history will judge him gently and see him in a favorable perspective. He did have a feeling for American problems, for poverty, for the disinherited and disadvantaged. During his presidential campaign in 1964 he used to draw rude snickers when he would say, in his flagrant manner, that he knew something about poverty. He knew what it was to shine shoes and work for a dollar a day. He knew what it was to be hungry. It was incongruous. The big Texan, strong, powerful, a multimillionaire who lived at the peak and in the manner of some potentate of old, surrounded by servants (and some thought sycophants), seemed anything but a man out of poverty. But Lyndon was more than a bombastic Texas stereotype. He did sense personal problems, he did understand and try to alleviate them. At the least, we think he will be regarded as one of our most tragic Presidents.

It was his fate to preside at a time when old values were changing, when new forces were rising, when society and government were under severe challenge, when the progressive or populist voice no longer was adequate to the moment.

He spoke as an American primitive and left a legacy as an American original. He was both great and gross, full of promise and imperfections. He did more than the country realized or appreciated, and accomplished less than his own dreams.

In that, Lyndon Johnson was like America itself.

Photo Credits

Index

BJ674H

Harwood.

   Lyndon.

BJ674H

Harwood.

   Lyndon.

January 1974